SAKURA

Cherry Blossom Paintings by Yoshiko Ishikawa

SAKURA

Cherry Blossom Paintings by

Yoshiko Ishikawa

The National Museum of Women in the Arts, Washington, D.C.

March 4 — April 11, 1993
The National Museum of Women in the Arts, Washington, D.C.

Organized by
The National Museum of Women in the Arts

Supported by
The Japanese Embassy in the U.S.A.

Financially supported by
The Japan Foundation
The Kajima Foundation for the Arts

With the cooperation of
Japan Airlines

ISBN 0-940979-22-5
Library of Congress Catalogue Card Number : 92-62884

Contents

Acknowledgments 7
Rebecca Phillips Abbott

On the Occasion of the Yoshiko Ishikawa Exhibition 9
Michiaki Kawakita

The Path of Flowers 11
Keinosuke Murata

The Revealing Strength of Yoshiko Ishikawa's Art 20
Alik Cavaliere

This Bewitching Flower 25
Ayako Sono

Exhibition Checklist 96

Chronology 99

Books Illustrated by Yoshiko Ishikawa 107

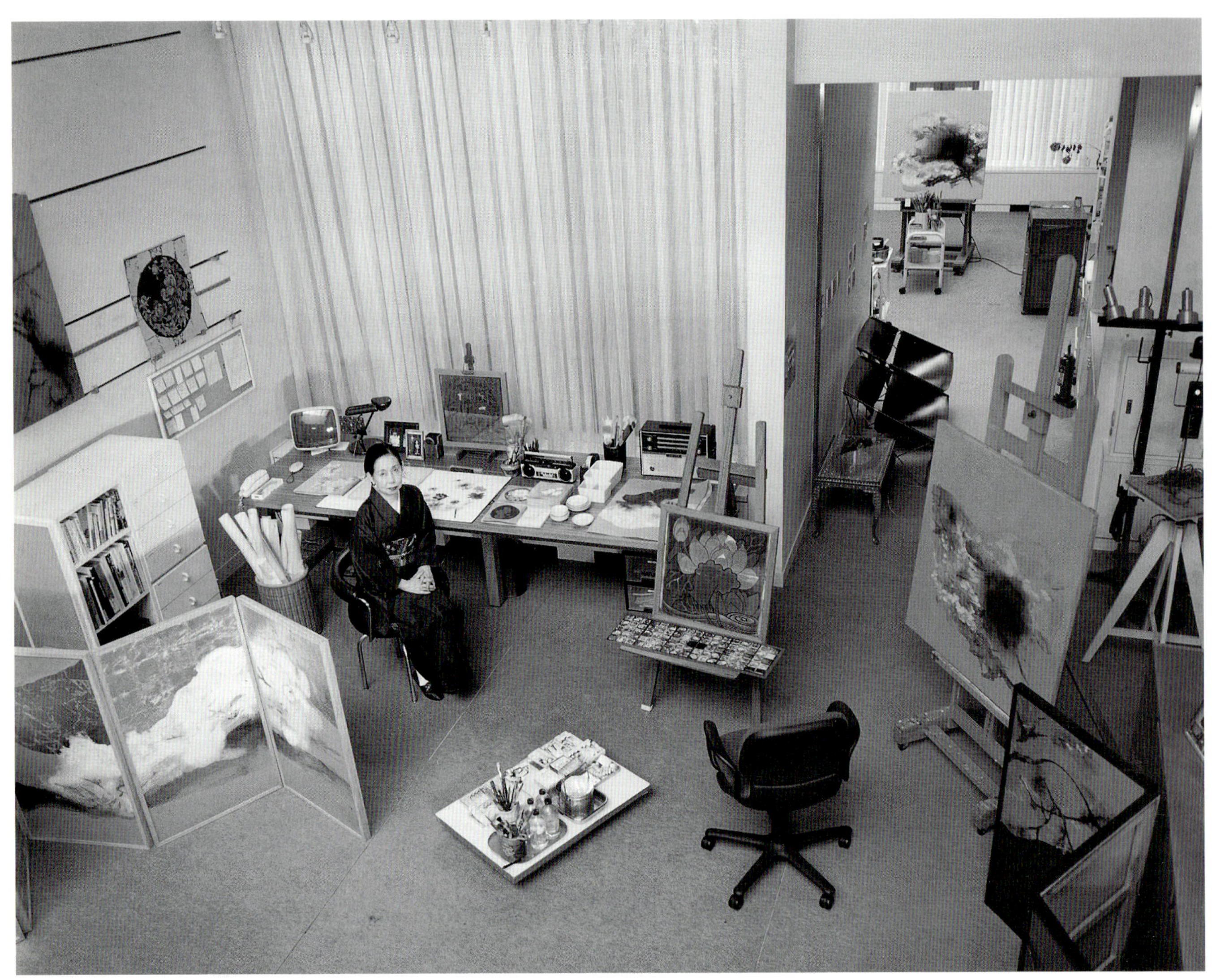

In her atelier, Tokyo 1992

Acknowledgments

The friendship between the United States and Japan has long been associated with the beauty of the cherry blossom tree. In 1912 3,000 trees arrived in Washington from Tokyo, a gift from the Japanese people to First Lady Helen Taft. Since then the delicate white blossoms of the *Akebono* trees and pale pink flowers of the *Yoshino* have decorated the Tidal Basin in our nation's capital, becoming a treasured emblem of spring for Washington residents, as well as for countless visitors from across the country and around the world.

Through the years Washington's cherry blossom trees have proven to be a source of both pride and passionate concern. During the 1940s, when it became clear that many of the trees encircling the Tidal Basin would have to be moved to make way for the Jefferson Memorial, cherry blossom enthusiasts chained themselves to the tree trunks, while others occupied the holes left by the trees that had been uprooted. In 1965 the United States was pleased to be able to return the gift of cherry blossoms, sending cuttings from its own trees to Tokyo to replenish Japan's native stocks.

The National Museum of Women in the Arts is particularly gratified, therefore, that the principal theme of this, its third exhibition of Japanese art, is the cherry blossom tree itself. The museum is honored to have the opportunity to present the show *SAKURA Cherry Blossom Paintings by Yoshiko Ishikawa.*

Every painting in this exhibition attests to the keen insight with which Yoshiko Ishikawa views nature, at all times of day and during every season of the year, and demonstrates the remarkable artistry she has achieved as a flower painter. It is this union of sensitivity and technical skill which has enabled Ishikawa to capture the essence of the cherry blossom in all its transient beauty.

We thank all who have helped NMWA develop this beautiful show and catalogue. We are grateful to Yoshiko Ishikawa herself for her ongoing interest in the exhibition and in the museum. We are grateful to art critic Keinosuke Murata, former chief curator of the National Museum of Art, Osaka, who has been instrumental in curating and organizing the exhibition, as well as preparing the catalogue. We thank the catalogue essayists ··· art critic Michiaki Kawakita, former director of the National Museum of Modern Art, Kyoto;

sculptor Alik Cavaliere, former dean of the Brera Academy of Fine Arts in Milan; and Ayako Sono, one of Japan's most prominent novelists. We also would like to thank those at the Nichido Museum of Art Foundation in Tokyo who have been kind enough to help us develop the exhibition, particularly Chieko Hasegawa, vice-president of the foundation.

A final note of thanks goes to Lily Y. Tanaka, a valued member of our Board of Directors and an unfailing supporter of the museum. It is only due to Mrs. Tanaka's diligence and enthusiasm that NMWA has been successful in developing a series of exhibitions with Japan since the summer of 1990, and we are extremely grateful.

Rebecca Phillips Abbott
Director for Administration

On the Occasion of the Yoshiko Ishikawa Exhibition

Michiaki Kawakita

Art Critic
former Director of The National Museum of Modern Art, Kyoto

It was with great pleasure that I heard of the coming exhibition of my longtime acquaintance Yoshiko Ishikawa at The National Museum of Women in the Arts in Washington D.C. Based primarily on the theme of *sakura*, Japan's flowering cherry, the exhibition will consist of eighteen oil paintings, fourteen works in pastel and one tapestry. Having seen the outstanding show from the collection of The National Museum of Women in the Arts that toured Japan from 1990 to 1991, it makes us, Ishikawa's supporters in Japan, very proud to hear of her solo show at this museum, which comes in the wake of the recent Setsuko Migishi exhibition. We believe the Ishikawa exhibition offers another view, from an entirely different perspective, of the quality of work being produced today by Japanese women in the arts.

When viewing the works of Yoshiko Ishikawa, there are two points to which I hope the viewer will give particular attention. The first is that Ishikawa is an excellent painter of her favorite subject, flowers. Coinciding with the upcoming 1993 Cherry Blossom Festival, this exhibition consists largely of works on the theme of sakura, one of Japan's representative flowers. Ishikawa uses her full repertoire as a painter of flowers to place the sakura in a variety of natural settings and conditions. In some instances she paints the cherry blossoms at the height of their flowery beauty, while in other paintings they may be portrayed with a more dramatic touch. Her sakura may be wrapped in the misty beauty of a rainy day, blown before the wind in a flurry of petals or bathed in the glow of evening light.

When Ishikawa paints sakura or one of her many other flower motifs, her work always contains some expression of the subtle nuances that color the Japanese environment, whether it be the progression of the seasons from spring through summer and fall to winter or the changing light from morning to evening. We cannot fail to see the sincerity with which the artist's eye watches the lives of these children of nature, as they bud, blossom and eventually fall.

Another aspect of her work which must not be overlooked is the sureness of her technique and the rich originality of her methods of expression. Professor Alik Cavaliere of Milan's Brera Academy of Fine Arts, who knows Ishikawa's art well, has described her work as "paintings of strength and intelligence." Here, strength surely refers to the bold, expressive flair of her brushwork and use of paint, while intelligence describes the distinct skill and sober calculation with which she matches technique and subject, as well as the depth of culture and refinement that underlies all of her work.

I am in agreement with this opinion. Born in Rome and raised in a privileged Japanese family, Ishikawa is possessed of a uniquely warm and magnanimous blend of Eastern and Western culture and sensitivities. It is this kind of background and foundation, I believe, that has helped her to bloom into the fine woman of the arts we see today.

Regardless of where its origins might lie, I feel in her work the presence of a brilliant blending of the strong structural qualities of Western oil painting and the fluid grace of the Eastern painting tradition that breathes life and motion into her art. Within this blending we can find traditional expressions of permeation and space, as well as the decorative brilliance of such 17th-century masters as Sōtatsu Tawaraya and Kōrin Ogata. We can also see the presence of contemporary abstract expression. Of course, the total result cannot be classified within the confines of any of these traditions and must surely be recognized as the singular achievement of the artist herself. Above all, I hope the viewer will appreciate how devotedly the artist, in her strong and intelligent way, pursues the life cycles of her flowers in search of the true face of nature itself.

In closing, I would like to express my hope that this exhibition of the works of Yoshiko Ishikawa will be an opportunity for all who see it to reflect once again on the importance of the fragile life embodied in all the flowers of the earth.

The Path of Flowers

Keinosuke Murata

Art Critic
former Chief Curator of The National Museum of Art, Osaka

The tradition of using flowers as a subject of art goes far back in Japanese history. The *Man'yōshū*, Japan's ancient poetry collection dating from the middle of the 8th century, contains some 4,500 poems. Among them we find mention of well over one hundred different species of plants, including about fifty types of flowers. The flowers referred to most often by the *Man'yōshū* poets are the plum blossoms and bush clover, with all other flowers, notably the camellia and cherry blossoms, making up less than half the total.

Of all flowers, it was the plum blossoms that the privileged class of the 8th century in Japan mentioned most frequently in their poetry. This fact is considered largely to reflect the Chinese literati's preference for this flower at a point in history when Japanese culture was still heavily influenced by that of its advanced neighbor to the west.

As was the case in China, plum blossoms were loved in Japan for their fragrance. Entering the Heian Period (9th—11th centuries), however, we find courtiers who once adorned themselves with plum blossoms in the spring choosing cherry blossoms instead. In time, with the emergence of a truly indigenous Japanese culture, the cherry came to stand alone among all flowers, to the point that the word flower itself became synonymous with the blossoms of the cherry. This poetic convention remains true to this day.

Even as this transition was taking place, however, such master artists of the Muromachi Period (14th—16th centuries) as Sesshū, still used the plum as his preferred subject. The painting tradition on which Sesshū and other Muromachi Period masters based their art was derived from Song Period Chinese painting styles transported to Japan along with the spiritual influences of Zen Buddhism.

For this exhibition Yoshiko Ishikawa has chosen *sakura* (cherry blossoms) as her main theme. The fact that the exhibition takes place in Washington during cherry blossom season was, perhaps, a factor in this choice, but I am also certain that she was extremely conscious of the traditional Japanese aesthetics involving cherry blossoms in making her selection. Of course, this is not the first time that Ishikawa has painted cherry blossoms, and there will be some earlier paintings exhibited along with the new works.

As suggested above, cherry blossoms have long been an important motif in Japanese art. They have been the subject of numerous masterpieces in traditional Japanese Nihonga painting, executed in mineral pigments mixed with glue. Rarely have attempts been made at this motif by Japanese painters working in oils, however, a medium that entered Japan along with other elements of European culture just over one hundred years ago. Perhaps the lack of modern oil paintings of cherry blossoms can be explained, in part, by the fact that, even today, as we are finally emerging from a dark period of our country's history, cherry blossoms as an artistic motif still carry a stigma from the days when they were used by the misguided forces of Japanese nationalism. In the early part of this century the cherry blossom was a symbol of distinctly Japanese culture involving an aesthetic of fleeting beauty and the transience of life. For example, the saying "the flower is [epitomized by] the cherry tree, man is [epitomized by] the samurai" is no more than an expression of two aspects of hierarchy in Japanese feudal life. There is a danger, however, of its being misinterpreted as a suggestion that both the flowers and men (warriors) achieve their greatest glory at the moment of death.

Aside from such considerations, it should also be noted that cherry blossoms are by no means an easy subject to paint. When considered from the standpoint of material and method, we find that interpretation of cherry blossoms as a subject of painting goes beyond mere differences in medium or technique, involving the very way one sees or feels about the subject. The fact that traditional *kosai* (glue painting) renderings of cherry blossoms appear to conform to certain models is due, in part, to the restrictions imposed by the medium and techniques used. Their seeming conformity is also due to a concept shared by a number of traditional Japanese arts, such as Noh theater —the concept that artistic challenge lies in making the fullest possible use of certain patterns or models while working within a set of carefully delineated conventions governing the artform. This approach offers the possibility for new creative expression, yet guarantees the preservation of the artistic tradition.

Within the kosai tradition cherry blossoms are usually painted in such a manner that, in extreme cases, it appears as if a single stamp was used to create identical impressions of blossoms along a branch, or petals across the ground. This may explain why traditional artists preferred the mountain cherry as a

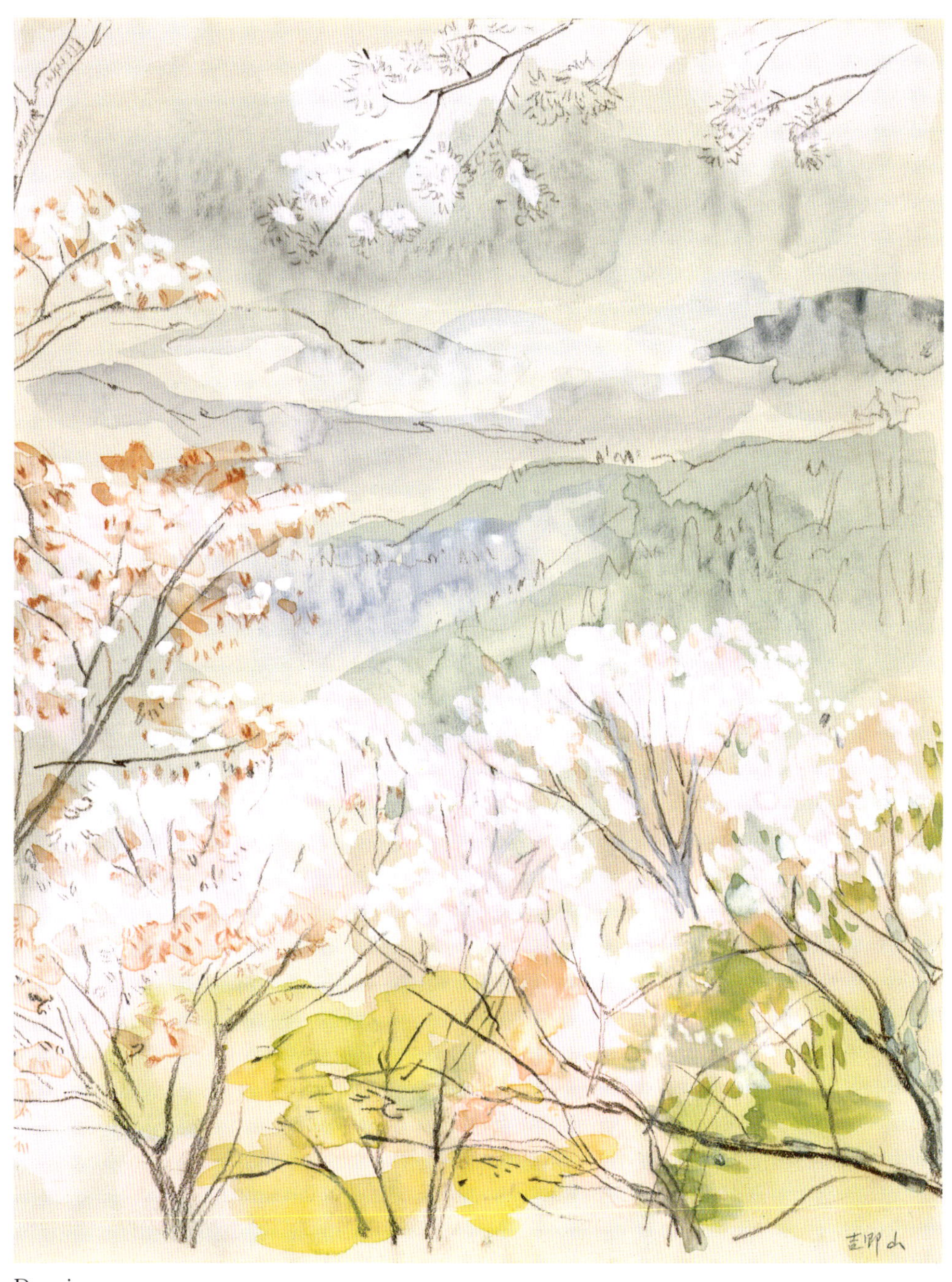

Drawing
Gouache on paper. 16 1/8 × 12 5/8 inches. 40.8 × 32 cm.

subject, with its simple five-petal blossoms, to other, more elaborate, strains of the tree. Although the aesthetic was limited to the literati of a certain period in Japanese history, the mountain cherry came to be perceived in terms of a prescribed format encompassing the entire flower cycle—from the first opening of the blossoms to their full bloom, and then proceeding, like some Buddhist ceremony, to the falling and scattering of the petals. In another convention cherry trees in full bloom are portrayed from a distance in long stands that reduce the individual trees to misty clouds in which the floral patterns are submerged in a field of delicate pink.

Over time the appeal of these formalized representations of the flowers moved from the visual to the conceptual realm. In literature the conceptual aspects of the blossoms has been expressed most cleary perhaps in the collection of essays known as the *Tsurezure-gusa* by 14th-century author Kenkō Yoshida. "Should we look at the cherries only in full bloom and the moon only at its brightest?" he writes. He goes on to say, "Should we be so thoughtless as to look at the moon and the cherry blossoms only with our eyes? Staying indoors on a spring day or in one's bedchamber on a moonlit night and thinking of the cherry blossoms or the moon is also a poetic and amusing way to occupy oneself." When one tries to see such objects as cherry blossoms strictly in a visual context, there is a tendency for only the outer framework of the tradition to remain. In other words, there is a danger in assuming that cherry blossoms are a thing of beauty and allowing one's perceptions to be guided by the preconceived conventions that have come to stand as symbols of the traditional aesthetic. Certainly, the cherry tree in bloom is a thing of beauty, but the traditional concepts must always be referenced first to elements from the real world.

When we look for examples of cherry blossoms as a theme in the oil painting tradition, we find one of the few significant precedent to be that of Mitsuo Shirane (b.1926), who painted the mountain cherry almost exclusively for over ten years. Unfortunately, this important motif and theme has been avoided or abandoned by most other artists working in oil. Shirane chose as his subject the famous cherry-viewing spot, Mt. Yoshino, where mountain cherry covers the slopes for nearly as far as the eye can see. He portrayed the unique atmosphere of illusion created by the waves of cherry trees in full bloom—one that borders on the psychological abyss of obsession—in an ornamental, two-dimensional style. Using this approach, he sought to restore the tradition of the recurring Japanese aesthetic surrounding the cherry blossom that had been partially lost in the refracted vision of the World War II generation.

In this case, obsession means being possessed by the flowers, not the kind of mental state which eventually leads to derangement. From the Edo Period (17th—19th centuries) we have the story of a painter from Kyoto whose love of cherry blossoms was so great that he devoted his entire career to painting them, even choosing Kaden, meaning "one possessed by flowers," as his pseudonym. Upon his death his friends took instruction from a poem he left behind and threw his cremated remains into a waterfall at one of his beloved cherry-viewing spots. In modern literature we find the authors Motojiro Kajii (1901–32) and Ango Sakaguchi (1906–55) making use of the animistic sentiments that a cherry in full bloom evokes in the Japanese by employing the trees as vehicles for spirits or transfigurations in their writings.

Whereas Shirane's art evolves from a spatial sense of perception, Ishikawa's expression is based on a sense of time in which lyricism is allowed to develop freely. Her forms expand or congregate with the passage of time, but the lyricism does not evolve easily. On the contrary, she manages to weave her patterns of beauty while revealing to us the sharp cutting edge of time. It is here that we seem to hear the persistent voice deep in the soul that suppresses the artistic urge to give oneself up to obsession. Ishikawa constructs paintings that resist the unconscious patterning of subject, the separation from reality and the loss of spatial continuity that have been the pitfalls of traditional art. By doing so she succeeds in rendering sincere expressions of the ephemeral beauty of the cherry blossoms, captured poetically in such classical lines as, "now in such full bloom they seem fragrance" or "is it mist, clouds, as far as the eye can see." The paintings of Ishikawa's that incorporate the technique of bleeding colors comparable to that used in traditional Japanese painting and express a strong sense of the transience underlying a seemingly mundane contemplation of subject I would like to call a type of lyrical realism.

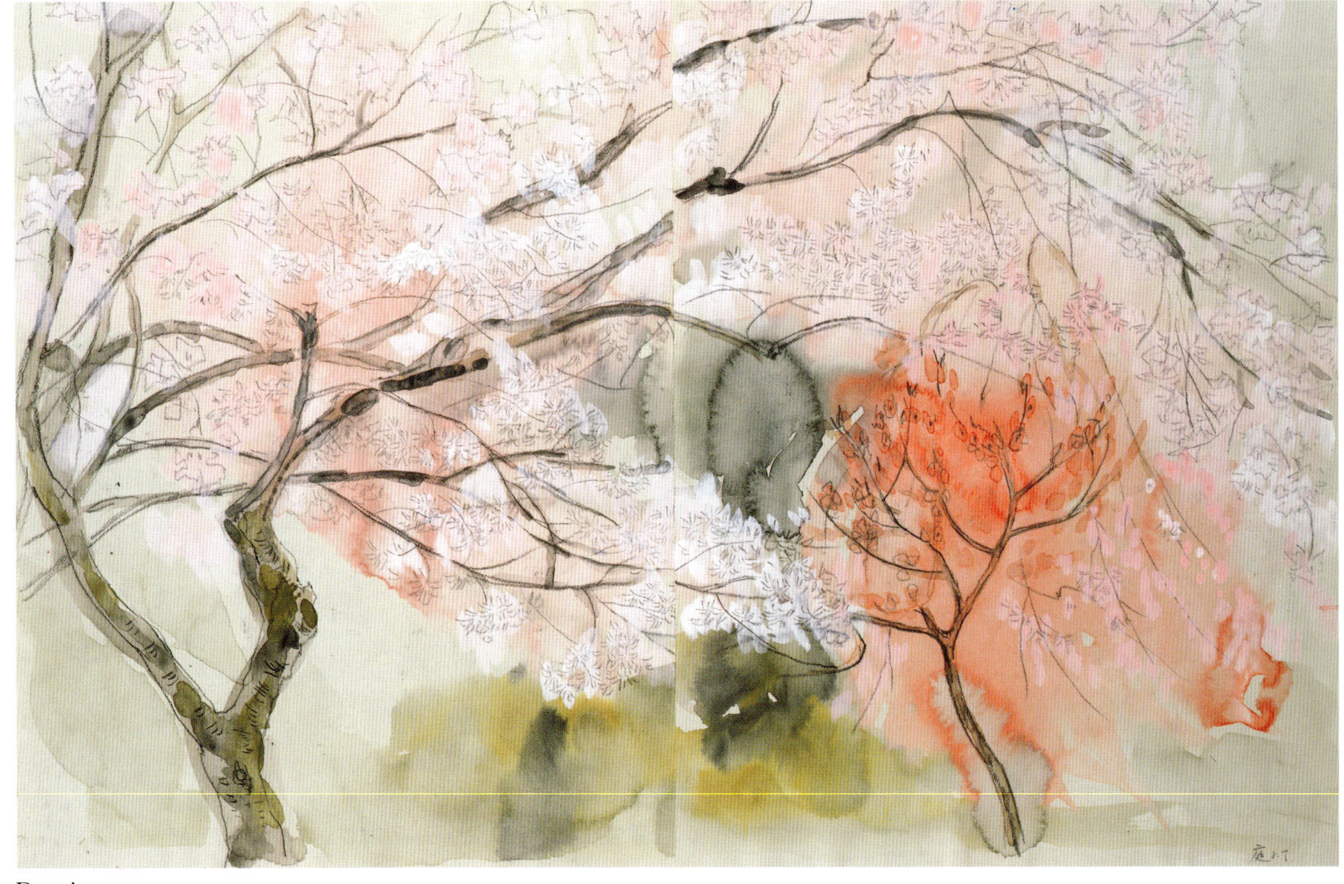

Drawing
Gouache on paper. 16 1/8 × 25 1/4 inches. 40.8 × 64 cm.

Shasei (drawing) in the Japanese or, more correctly, the oriental tradition, has always involved more than the simple representation of the subject. It also includes an effort by the artist to perceive the life-essence of the subject, and create an image that creates a vehicle for the expression of the artist's own essence. If shasei can only be translated into English as realism, then the realism of Ishikawa's work must be defined as a very oriental form in which the psychological perspective brought to bear on the subject results in the mutual expression of life-essence.

Ishikawa by no means paints flowers of illusion. The bleeding or blurring of the colors is not intended to create an illusionary effect, but rather to express the gentle passage of time that measures the life flowing between herself and her flowers. Having once studied the type of European realism that did not exist in Japanese tradition but maintaining her own personal style, the artist was able one day, through the vehicle of flowers, to discover the realism that has been nurtured by the Japanese tradition.

A major difference in the method of achieving realism in western and Japanese art lies in the degree to which the entire surface of a work is painted in. In oriental art, the portions that are not painted, the so-called empty space, are not thought to subtract from the image; rather, they constitute a positive element with the potential to carry a variety of meanings and images. This oriental perspective on positive and negative space clarifies how Ishikawa intends her flowers to be positioned in her paintings. Although it appears at first that the flowers hold the central position in her compositions, in fact it is a combination of the flowers and the potent empty spaces that at times melt into them and at other times contrast with them that is the central element of her compositions. Interspersing the flowing shapes and colors with sensitive line in a style reminiscent of *sumi* painting, her works speak alternately of the strength and the gentleness of living things within the larger context of life's perpetual motion. When these compositions are compared to the allegorical paintings of flowers by Dutch painters of the 17th century, which also sought to portray the perpetual motion of life, the difference in approach becomes apparent.

In the Dutch paintings a few fallen flowers, scattered beneath a vase overflowing with full blooms from every season, were meant to convey the vanity of human pride. This kind of allegorical or metaphorical expression is also found in oriental art. In the case of Ishikawa, her paintings of bamboo are perhaps of this type. Unlike the conventional metaphor, however, in which the straight-growing bamboo is likened to a strong will that will not bend to wind or snow, Ishikawa divides the life of the bamboo into three parts which she titles *Shoot*, *Youth* and *Prime*, all the while looking through to the life-essence harbored within this stalwart grass. Her sensitivity to the life of plants is apparent not only in her bamboo paintings but also in her paintings of cherry blossoms shrouded in rain, falling in a flurry of petals or glowing mysteriously in night lighting. Whether she paints the blooms in spring, with their evocation of Eros, or the lovely, enclosed blossoms of winter, with their connotations of Thanatos, the works are always permeated with the artist's deep consciousness of the life-force that has brought them to bloom.

Ishikawa's autumn flowers are wrapped in an atmosphere of repose, but never sadness. As an artist who has followed the path of flowers, Ishikawa's perspective resembles somewhat the sentiment expressed by poet Bashō

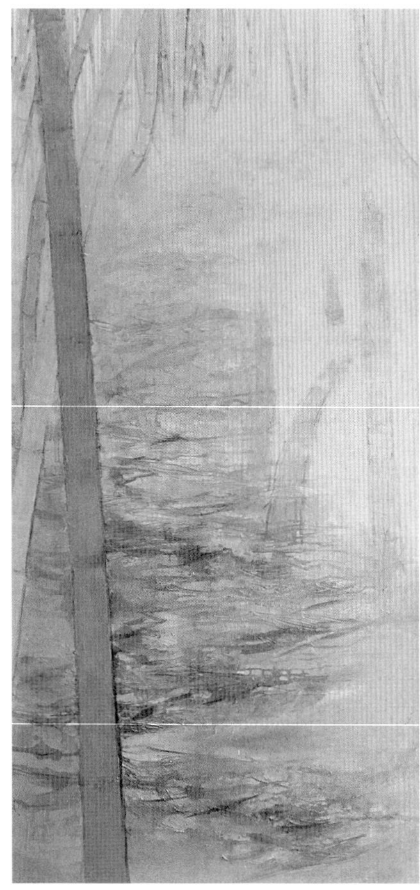

Bamboo (Shoot)
1981
Oil on canvas. 78 3/4 × 39 3/8 inches. 200 × 100 cm.

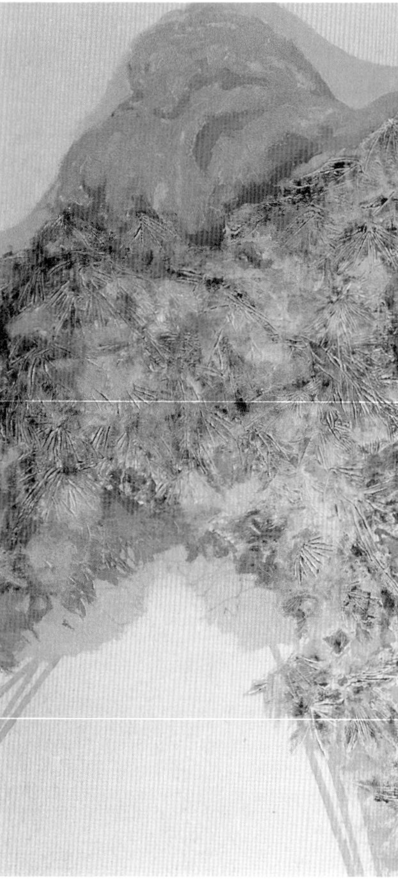

Bamboo (Youth)
1981
Oil on canvas. 78 3/4 × 39 3/8 inches. 200 × 100 cm.

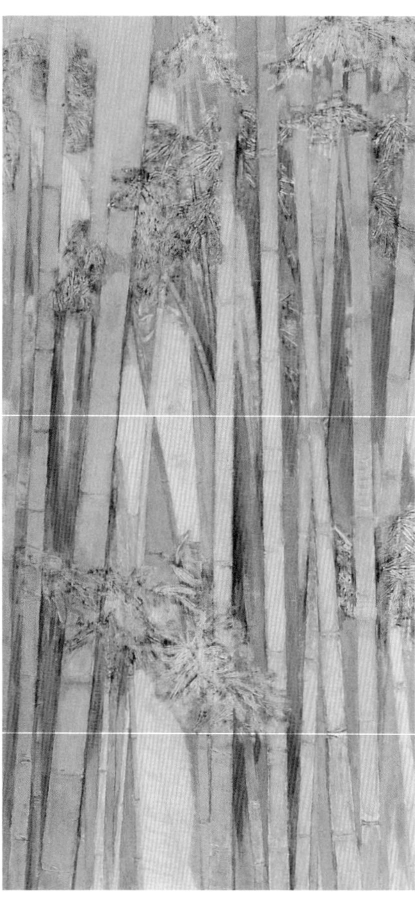

Bamboo (Prime)
1981
Oil on canvas. 78 3/4 × 39 3/8 inches. 200 × 100 cm.

Matsuo (1644—94), but certainly differs as well:

On this road
Not a single passerby
In autumn dusk.

Furthermore, she is an artist who will never reduce her subject to the level of object to such a degree as to place cut flowers in a vase and call the work a still life. In the case of the poetry and of the stylistic approach, Ishikawa's perspective differs because the flowers are still alive in the artist's mind.

The great Noh actor and playwright Zeami (ca.1364—1444) sought to express the essence of Noh with the word *hana* (flower). This flower, no matter how well it may be enacted on the stage within its prescribed forms, exists only in the feeling of newness and interest generated in the minds of the viewers. Destined as it is to be an artform based in time, it exists as a performance ultimately in the intellectual realm. This is why Zeami differentiated between *toki no hana* (momentary interest derived from the advantage of youth) and *makoto no hana* (true interest derived from a prolonged pursuit of discipline and innovation). Toki no hana was surely meant to characterize the excitement of a young actor's performance—like a momentary flower. Makoto no hana, which was like an eternal flower, was the interest generated by the performance of a fully matured actor. Although it may seem a bold statement, I believe that the flower given form in the work and the flower born in the mind can interact in the spatial and visual art of painting to create a path leading to makoto no hana. I believe that the paintbrush of Yoshiko Ishikawa, after long years of absorbing the Japanese tradition of artistic expression in her own pliant way, while nurturing the flowers of both the East and West as flowers of the mind, has opened a narrow but clear path of flowers.

The Revealing Strength of Yoshiko Ishikawa's Art

Alik Cavaliere

Sculptor
former dean of The Brera Academy of Fine Arts in Milan

The art of Yoshiko Ishikawa is both strong and intelligent. Strong in the way the paint is spread across the canvas, dominating it and transmitting its inner message with an immediacy that fascinates the viewer with moments of fusion and juxtaposition. What draws the artist and viewer together is more than just the lyricism of the work; there is also intense energy. The intelligence is in the use of the color, and texture, based on a depth of culture that is assimilated and filtered through the artist's talent and detached calculation.

These works speak to us through a single medium: flowers. In particular, we find the pervasive fragrance of the flowering cherry tree among her works. So strong is the presence of this delicate tree in Ishikawa's paintings that it seems we can almost taste the flavor of its fruit.

We find old memories of the cherry tree coming to mind. Brought from the orient in ancient times and nurtured with diligence and love by our Greek and Latin forebears, the cherry tree spread throughout the Western world. Today, it has become a natural part of our modern life, gracing our orchards and gardens with its delicate and joyous presence. The cherry also conjures up fond images in our collective cultural memory of ancient poets singing of the illusive color of its blossoms and tantalizing fragrance of its fruit. More recently, artists like Anton Chekhov and Giacomo Puccini have used the cherry tree to evoke nostalgia for past, happier times. In these paintings Yoshiko Ishikawa implants her own fascinating vision that goes beyond the attraction and nostalgia of these flowers, appealing to our eyes with resplendent images and luminous colors.

The symbolism of flowers is long and varied. Legend tells us that the most beautiful woman in the world, Lakshimi of India, was born of a flower. The Greeks and Romans used the term *sub rosa* (beneath the rose) as an expression of things secret and mysterious. The bloody War of the Roses raged on in 15th-century England for thirty years, with the opposing armies fighting under the banners of the white and the red rose.

In the mid-19th century, the most frequently reproduced artworks in Europe were the flower paintings of Antoine Redouté. These works were loved not only by emperors and queens but, through printed reproductions, by the general public as well. With reproduction, however, the value of the original works seemed to fade, along with the reputation of the artist himself, until he came to be known as no more than a genre painter. Finally, Redouté's name nearly disappeared from official critiques of recognized artists. The misunderstanding of the times was that painters who stuck to one theme, such as landscape, still life, portrait or nude, were second-class painters. (As if religious paintings, historical paintings or commemorative works did not constitute genre as well.)

Personally, I would prefer to simply look at a work for its own sake and gain from it what I can, rather than to become involved in discussions of the artist's personal history or subject matter. In fact, analyzing an artist's personal history or dealing analytically with each element, such as the subject, title and contents, invariably distances us to some degree from the work itself and the joy it can provide.

In the case of Yoshiko Ishikawa, however, there is such a strong integration of the person and the subject that it is nearly impossible not to consider the artist and her work together. As a painter, Ishikawa dissolves her soul into color and reveals her heart on every canvas. What is more, images of her personal history come through in the paintings as well. As a woman of the orient she is naturally immersed in the life of the East, but her works also show us her childhood images of the West, images transmitted largely through paintings.

The sum of all this is the transformation her flowers undergo. For Yoshiko Ishikawa, the blossoming of a flower is painting itself. Flowers blossom in color and light. They spread out across a surface, occupying it, assuming a life of their own, reincarnated, transformed. Now, removed from the flowers of our memory, these blossoms, newly created in paint, come to life once again before our eyes.

These are strong, intelligent paintings .....

The noble souls
of the Imperial abode,
in elegant leisure do,
Adorn themselves again today
with blossoms of sakura.

—Akahito Yamabe

Calligraphy by Takako Oishi

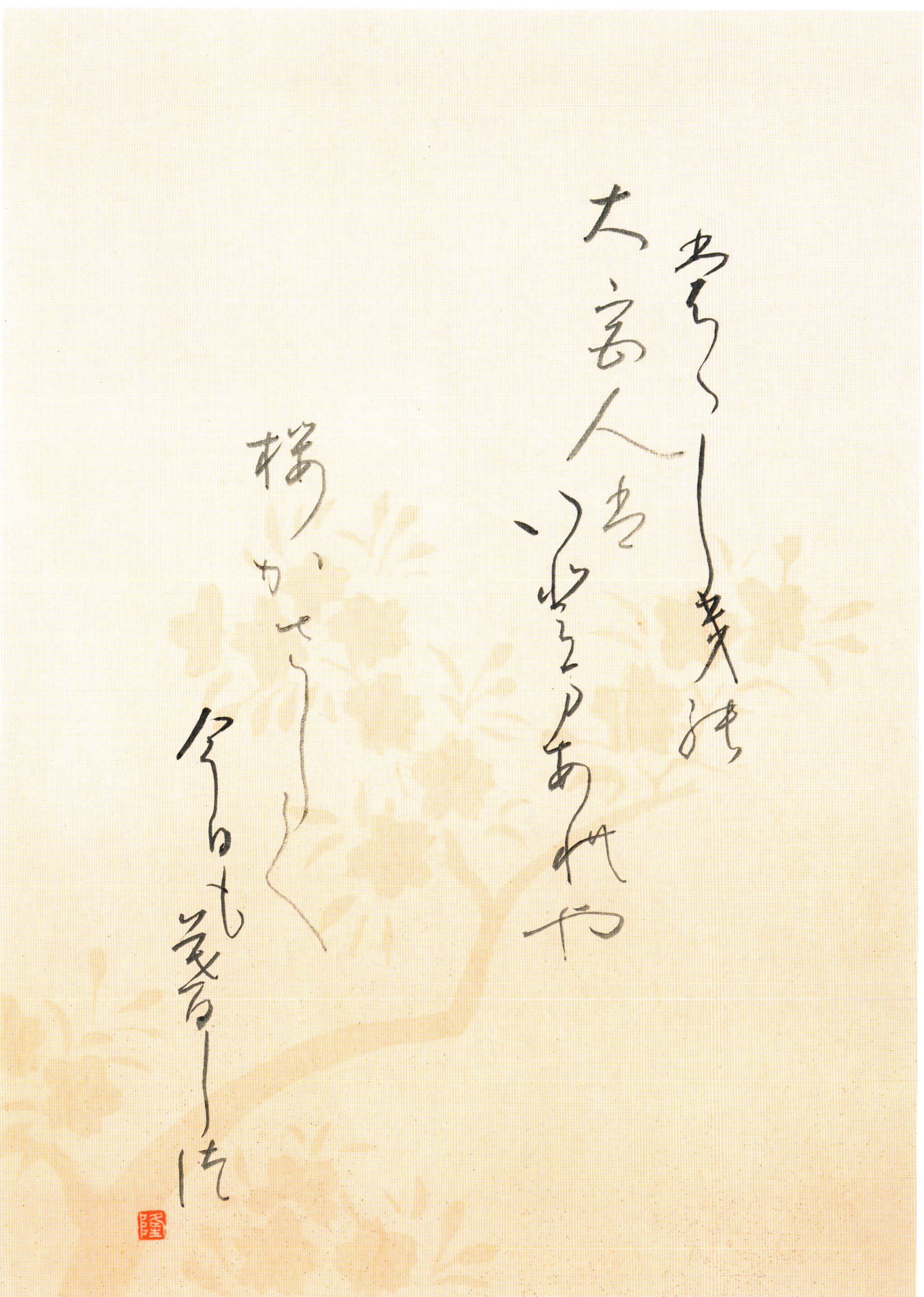

This Bewitching Flower

Ayako Sono

Novelist

As the central theme of this exhibition, Yoshiko Ishikawa has chosen to paint *sakura*, the flowering cherry. The meaning behind this choice certainly lies in the special significance the blossoms of the ornamental cherry tree hold for the Japanese, a subject which I would like to explore here.

The flowering cherry (which will be referred to here as sakura, the Japanese term meaning both the tree and its blossoms) is a tree that is found everywhere in Japan. In the spring, before its leaves appear, the tree is covered with a crown of pale pink blossoms. Its flower has five petals and blooms in clusters of three or four flowers that together measure about four centimeters (one and one-half inches) in diameter.

The most common variety of sakura, called *Somei yoshino*, can be seen everywhere, from remote mountainsides to urban residential areas. A grove of Somei yoshino in full bloom appears from a distance as heads draped in pink gauze, bringing the color of spring itself to the hills and towns.

What makes the sakura unique is the fact that it is only at the height of its beauty for a very short period of time. Perhaps in the West, there is a preference for things which retain their beauty for a long time, but in Japan we also cherish a deep sense of melancholy in the presence of the ephemeral. Sakura is probably at the height of its beauty for a period of only half a day to, at most, two days. If that day should see a change in weather, the sakura's moment of glory is shortened even more.

No sooner does the sakura reach full bloom than it begins to shed its blossoms. Torn away to dance on the wind or driven down by rain, the blossoms momentarily spread a pink carpet over the earth. As soon as the carpet been spread, it returns once again to soil. Sakura is by no means an ostentatious flower. Nonetheless, the splendid way in which it lives out its brief moment of glory and the innocence with which its petals fall have never failed to evoke fresh feelings and thought in the Japanese, down through the ages.

Last year I visited South Africa, at which time I could not help but notice the contrast between the South African national flower, the protea, and Japan's, the sakura. People in South Africa were surprised to learn that I have raised a protea bush in the garden of my seaside vacation home and thus am well acquainted with the nature of the flower.

Protea is a hardy flower that grows well even on weathered ground. If water is scarce, it survives on moisture stored in its thick leaves. Its large, bright vermilion flowers measure up to three to four centimeters across, and last for about a month. If cut, they can also be made into impressive dried flowers.

Sakura, on the other hand, has none of these qualities. Its petals scatter soon after blooming. The tree itself prefers the mountains and does not tolerate a sea breeze well. Its leaves are pliable and thin. In Japan we salt them to use as wrappings for a sweet called *sakura-mochi.* This delicacy is now an integral part of the Girl's Festival held every year on the third of March. I doubt that anyone would ever think of eating the leaves of the protea.

Since olden times, sakura has been associated with young maidens. The first appearance of sakura in Japanese writing goes back to the early part of the 8th century in a historical record called the *Nihon Shoki.* According to this record, the 5th-century Emperor Richū was enjoying a boating excursion on Ichishi no Ike, a pond in Iware, when a wind-borne petal of the sakura landed in his wine cup. So delighted was he by this chance occurrence, that the Emperor thereafter named his palace "Iware no Wakazakura no Miya" or, Palace of My Beloved Sakura of Iware. This incident speaks of the great importance the Japanese already attached to poetic things at this early stage in the nation's history.

A dozen or so years later, the Emperor Ingyō, without the knowledge of the Empress, was paying clandestine visits to his beloved, the young noble lady Sotoori no Iratsuhime. Legend has it that, early one morning after parting from his lover to return to the palace, the Emperor was struck by the beauty of a sakura in full bloom by a well and composed a poem comparing the beauty of his lady to its flowers.

Among the nobility of the court of Yamato, as ancient Japan was known, the sakura was the representative flower. We find the classical poetry collections of ancient and feudal Japan, the *Man'yōshū* (ca.738), *Kokinshū* (ca.905) and *Shin-Kokinshū*(ca.1205), filled with verses by poets inspired by sakura. Its flowers are always portrayed as a thing of beauty that soon falls victim to untimely wind or snow, however. People saw the sakura as the most immediate metaphor for the transience of the world.

Yononaka ni
taete sakura no
nakariseba
haru no kokoro wa
nodoke karamashi.

Imagine, if you will,
a world completely rid
of the sakura and its flower:
Free we would be then to spend
our Springs with peace of mind.
— Narihira Ariwara (9th century)

Hisakata no
hikari nodokeki
haru no hi ni
shizu kokoro naku
hana no chiruran.

As light from the heavens
bathes all in tranquility
on this spring day,
Surely it is with unsettled hearts
these blossoms fall and scatter.
— Tomonori Ki (ca. 10th century)

Yoshinoyama
sakura ga eda ni
yuki chirite
hana osogenaru
toshi nimo arukana.

On Mount Yoshino,
sakura boughs dusted white
alas, with snow,
Telling me the blossoms
will be late again this year.
— Saigyō (12th century)

Here is the equivalent of the saying "a beauty's moment is short-lived." We sense a fateful acceptance of the fact that happiness soon gives way to grief. For lovers to be kept apart for reasons such as a difference in class, political intrigue or illness seems to have been an unavoidable fact of life in feudal times. We find the sakura often employed as a metaphor for the pity of such star-crossed love.

The nobles of the feudal court had a particular love for the sakura. We read that, in the court of the Shishinden Hall of the ancient palace, there were planted "a sakura on the left and a mandarin orange on the right." Both of these trees had an irreplaceable role in Japanese life and, as such, were ubiquitous throughout the country. In the strict hierarchy of the ancient court,

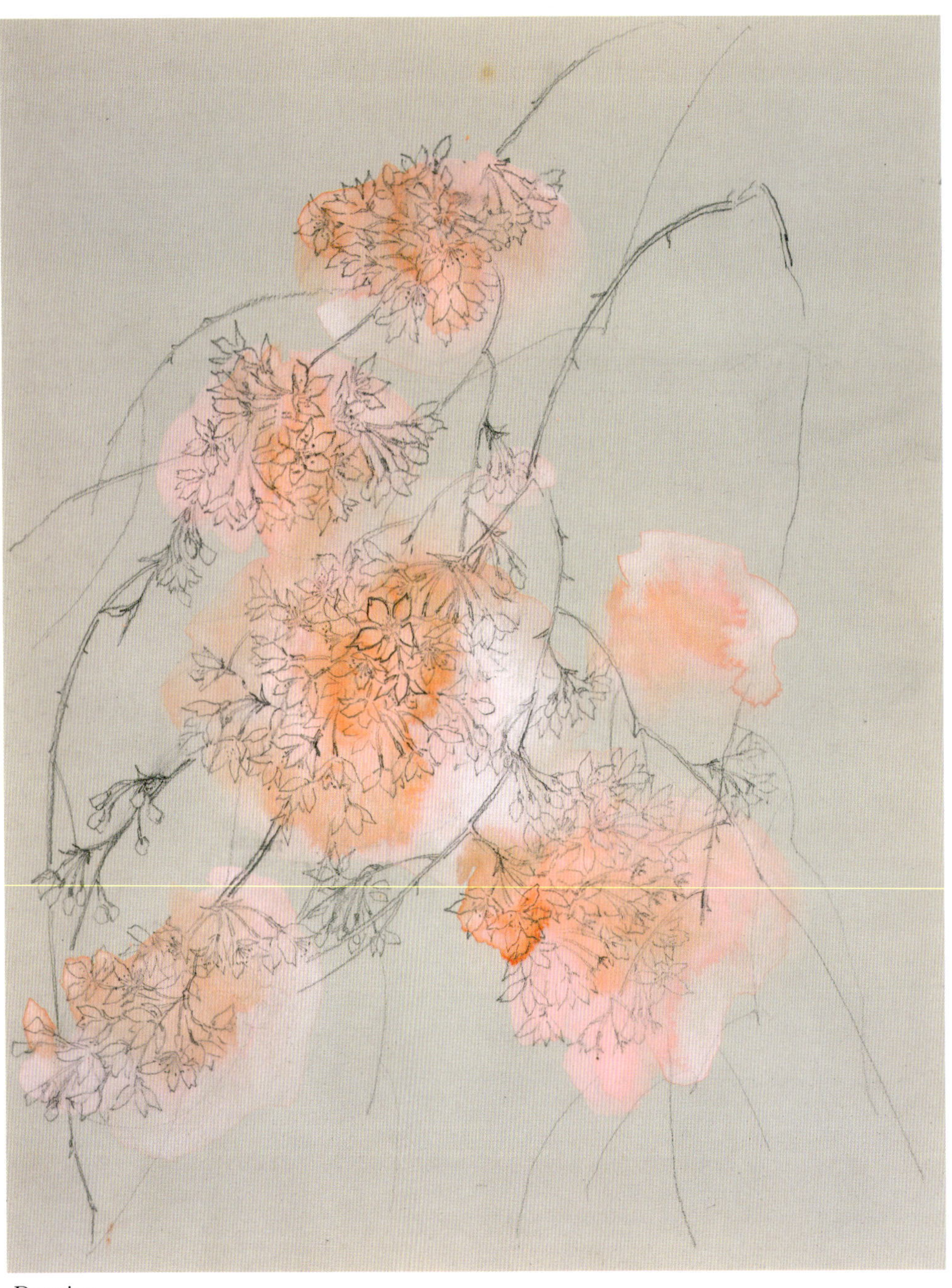

Drawing
Gouache on paper. 16 1/8 × 12 5/8 inches. 41 × 32 cm.

the left was always the position of superior rank; of the two, therefore, the sakura was held in higher esteem. We also know that, during its brief moment when the sakura bloomed each spring, the court nobility would adorn themselves with its blossoms. In the *Shin-Kokinshū* we find this fact expressed in the following verse:

Momoshiki no ōmiyabito wa itoma areya sakura kazashite kyō mo kurashitsu.	The noble souls of the Imperial abode, in elegant leisure do, Adorn themselves again today with blossoms of sakura. — Akahito Yamabe (ca. 8th century)

As the times changed and Japan's history entered the Muromachi Period (1336–1573) and later the Era of Warring States, sakura came to represent more than just pure beauty. Gradually it became a symbol expressing the harshness and cruelty of life. The winds of fortune shift, a capital lies in ruins, its people dead and gone, and only the sakura continues to bloom in all its glory. Here is a scene of piteous cruelty. The great 12th-century poet Tadanori Taira writes:

Sazanami ya Shiga no miyako wa arenishi o mukashi nagara no yamazakura kana.	Ripples on the water: over the sad ruins of the Shiga capital, The sakura still blooms with all the glory of those lost days.

The sakura always seemed to be attendant to the tragedy of human life. Even in its insentient form, the sakura seemed to offer sympathy to people in their moments of grief. After Takauji Ashikaga (1305–1358) established his Muromachi Regime, the Emperor Godaigo (1288–1339), realizing there was no longer a place for him in the seats of power, retired to the Temporary Palace at Mt. Yoshino. There he wrote:

Koko nite mo
  kumoi no sakura
    sakinikeri
tada karisome no
  yado to omouni.

Do my eyes behold
  sakura of the Cloud Residence
    blooming here in unrivaled glory;
Though I thought this no more
  than a transient abode.

The "Cloud Residence" refers to the sakura of the capital he has left behind. Near his Temporary Palace in Yoshino at the Yosonji Temple, the dethroned Emperor had found sakura in bloom to rival those of the Shishinden Hall of the palace he had left behind. For an outcast soul, this unexpected discovery was certainly a consolation and a gift to be humbly appreciated. If one were to choose a single poet who carried this usage of sakura as metaphor for the fleeting vanity of worldly life to the extremes of its poetic possibility, however, it would certainly be the priest Saigyō:

Negawakuwa
  hana no moto nite
    haru shinan
sono kisaragi no
  mochizuki no koro.

If wishes could be granted,
  would that I should die
    'neath the flowers in spring,
At the time of the full moon
  of the second month of the year.

It seemed a harsh reality of life that no sooner had one reached the full bloom of life than one fell victim to untimely death. If the flowers must fall (and here, as in Saigyō's poem, the word flowers, or *hana* in Japanese, is a poetic convention meaning the blossoms of the sakura), then how can a person complain about imminent death. Rather, isn't it best to die in a moment of rapture beneath the flowers ?

Norinaga Motoori (1730–1801), author of a spirited interpretation of the *Shin-Kokinshū* in which Saigyō's verse appears, was also a poet whose most famous verse is:

Shikishima no
yamatogokoro o
hito towaba
asahi ni niou
yamazakurabana.

Ask to know the spirit
of the noble days of Yamato
and my reply would be:
The blossoms of the mountain sakura
aglow with morning's light

Norinaga was a child left by his parents in the care of the Mikumari Shrinc in Yoshino, and considered himself to be something of an incarnation of the sakura (even asking that one be planted over his grave when he died). It was Norinaga, more than anyone else who consolidated the feelings about sakura sung by generations of poets into a firmly established part of Japanese culture.

Throughout all the eras of Japanese history, the sakura has always nurtured poetry and philosophy in the hearts and minds of the Japanese people. In this sense it is certainly a tree and a flower possessed of a unique and bewitching nature. Many are the painters, writers and dramatists who have become captivated by the uncanny allure of the sakura, struggling with and eventually discovering its spirit.

Now, Yoshiko Ishikawa is immersed once again in this quest for an important part of the Japanese soul. Yoshiko Ishikawa is the type of painter who wraps intensity in a cloak of tranquility, and this contradiction, in itself, can be considered another type of bewitchment. To be witness once again, through this exhibition, to the union of the painter's soul with the spirit of the sakura is a rare and precious opportunity for me, as I am sure it will be for you.

SAKURA

Cherry Blossom

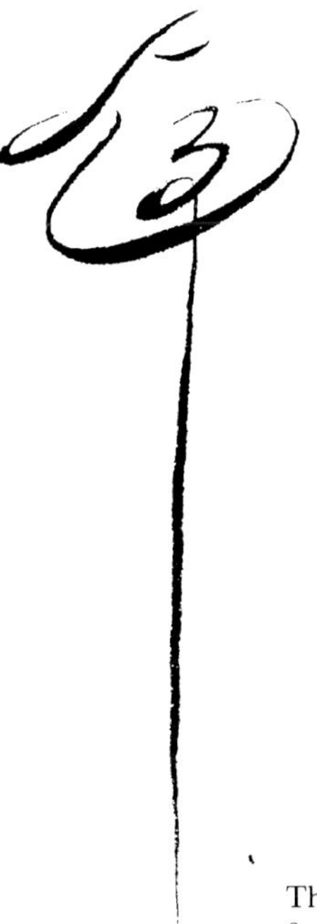

The artist's signature
for oil paintings

1

Winter (Icy Lake)

1984. Oil on canvas. 78 3/4 × 39 3/8 inches. 200 × 100 cm.

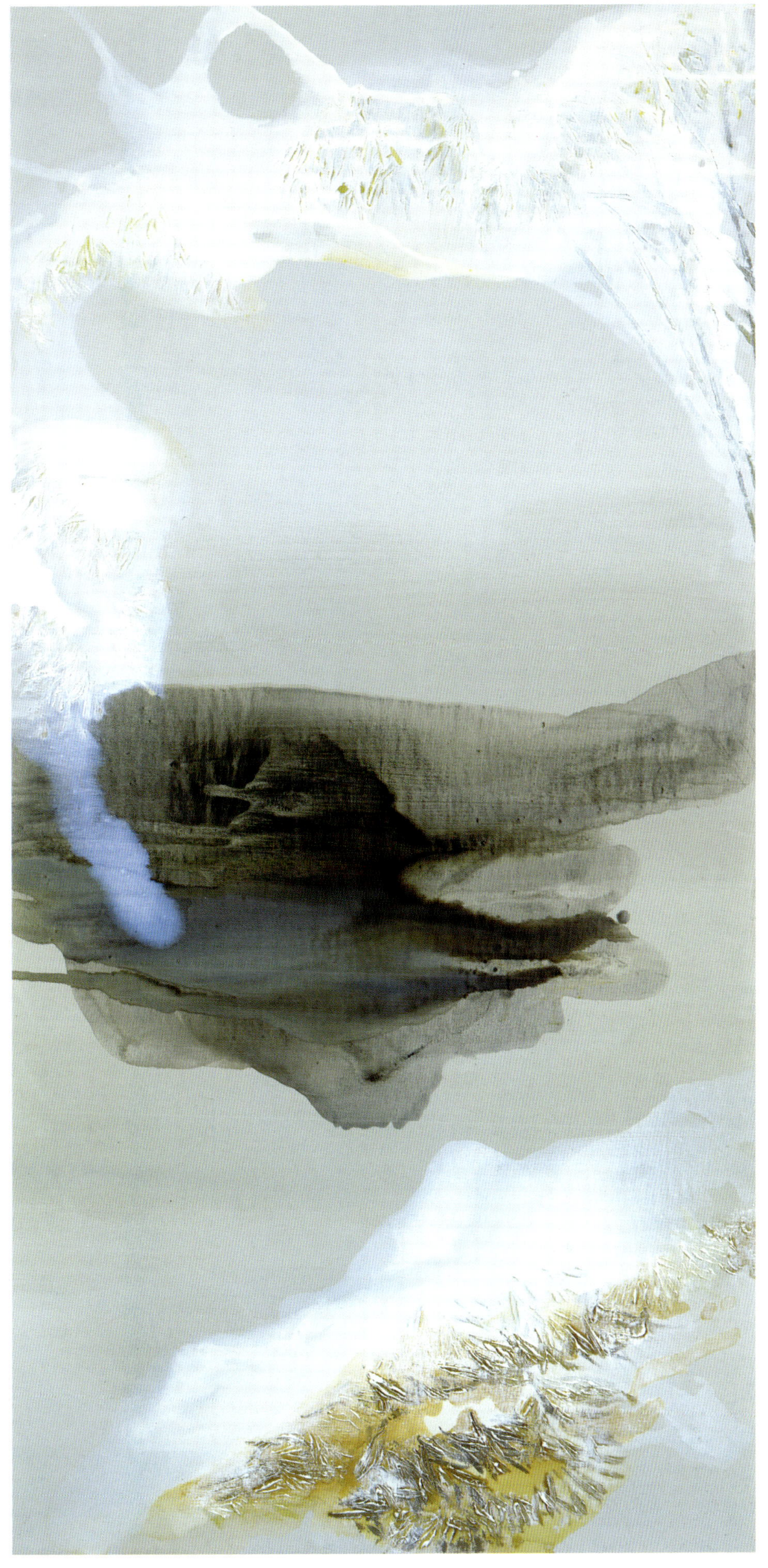

2

Winter (Flowers in the Snow)

1984. Oil on canvas. 78 3/4 × 39 3/8 inches. 200 × 100 cm.

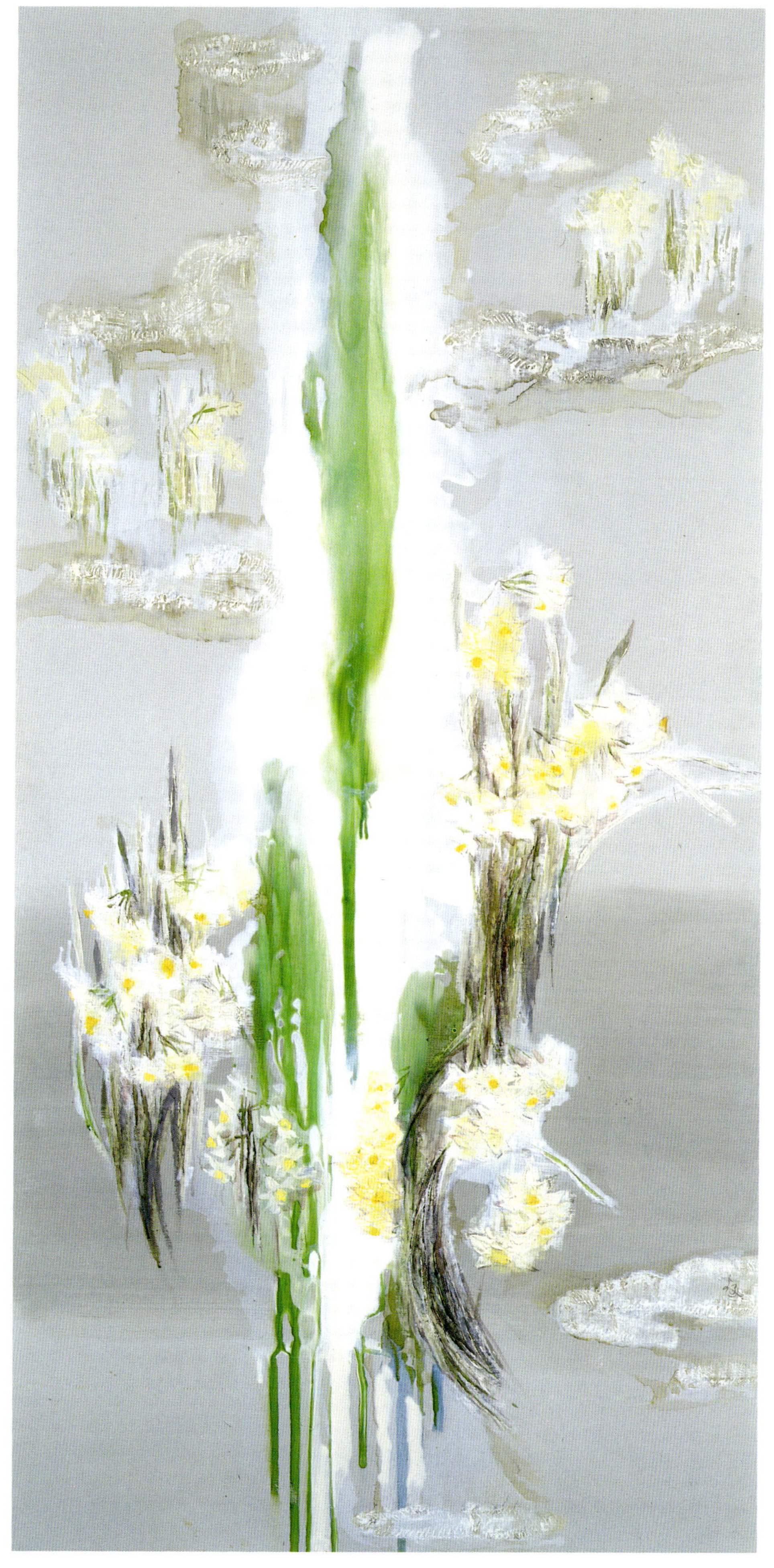

3

Winter (Deep Snow)

1984. Oil on canvas. 78 3/4 × 39 3/8 inches. 200 × 100 cm.

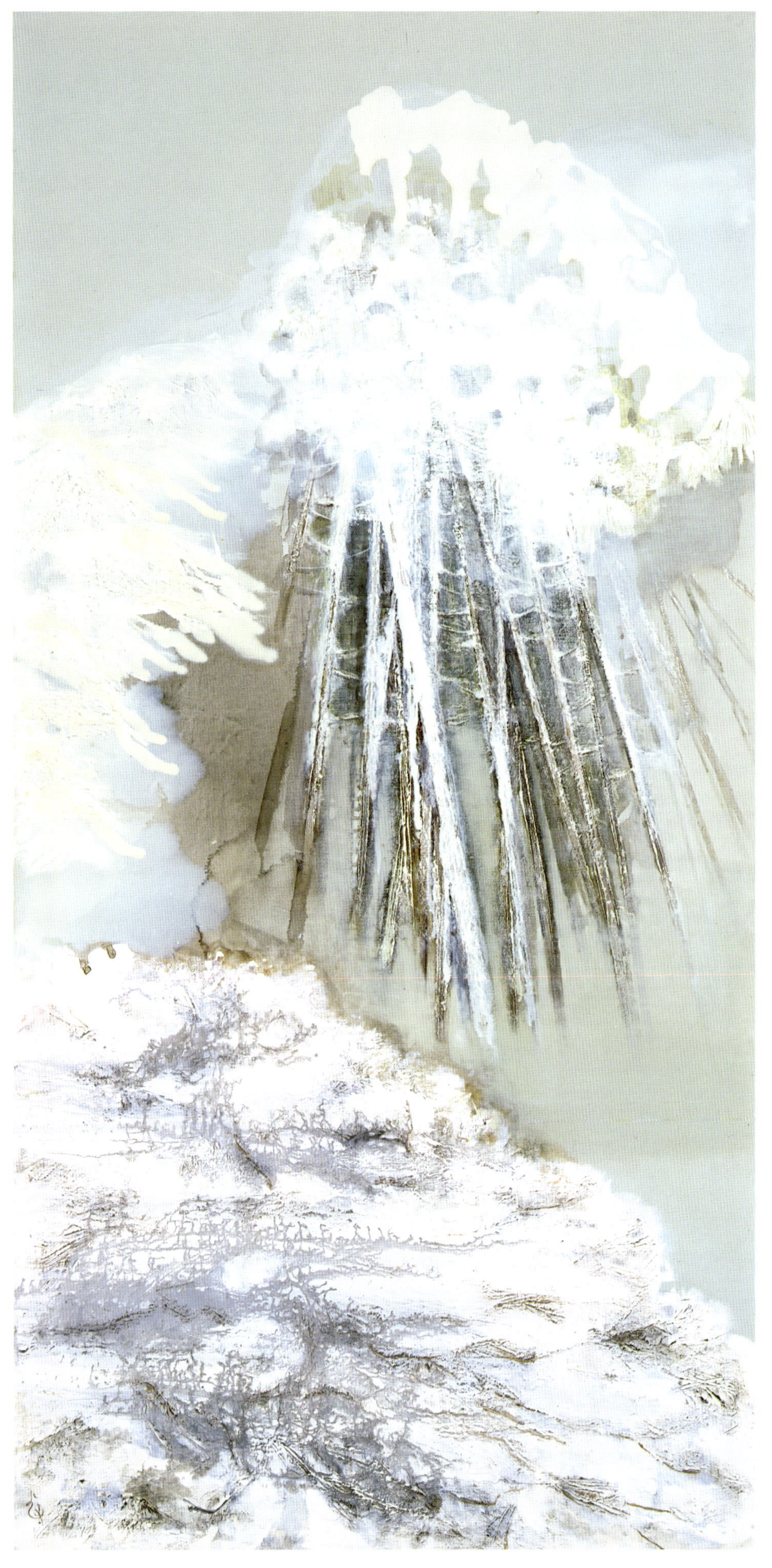

4

Spring (Amaryllis)

1984. Oil on canvas. $78\frac{3}{4} \times 39\frac{3}{8}$ inches. 200×100 cm.

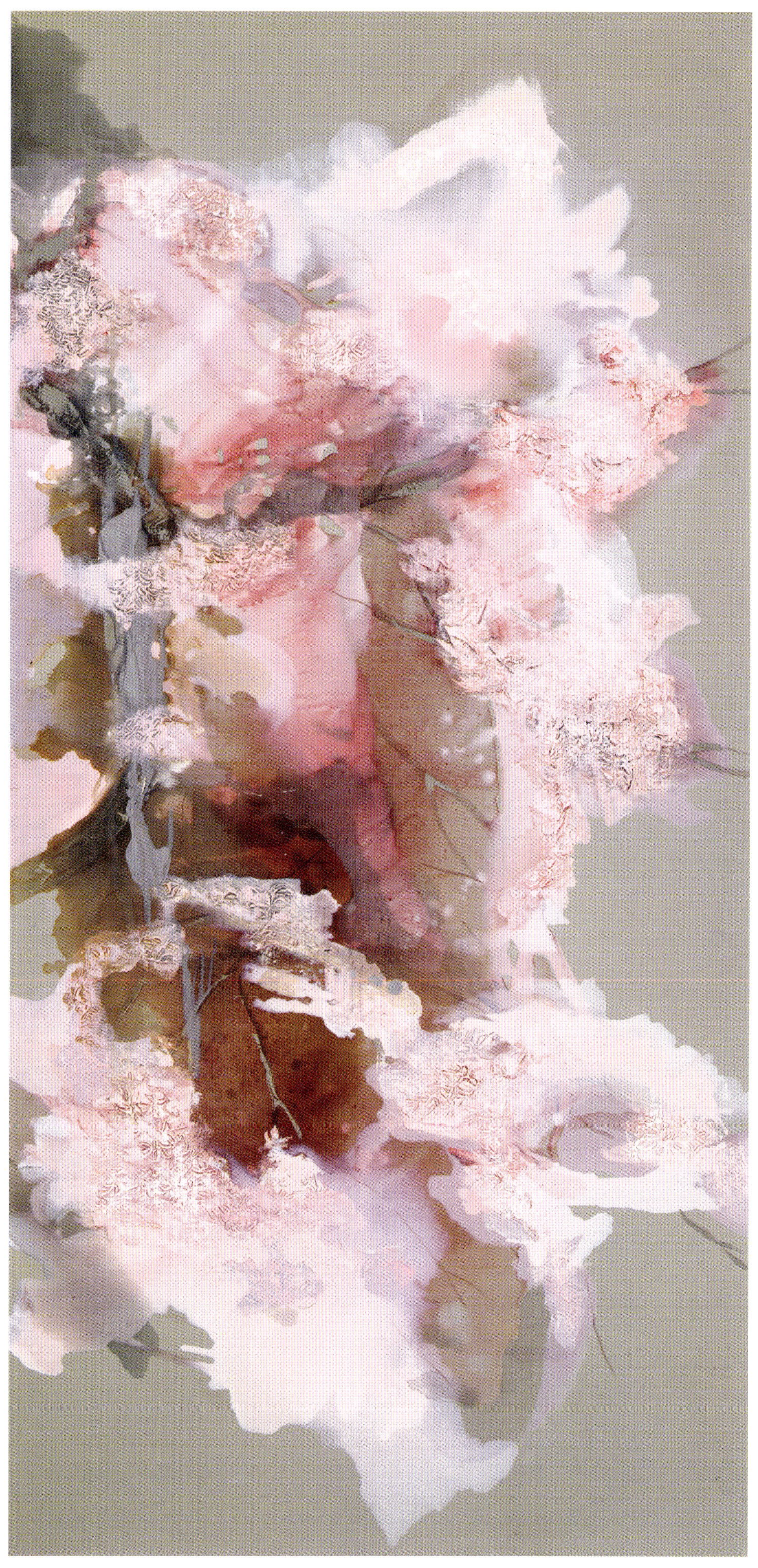

5

Spring (Cherry Blossoms at Night)

1984. Oil on canvas. 78 3/4 × 39 3/8 inches. 200 × 100 cm.

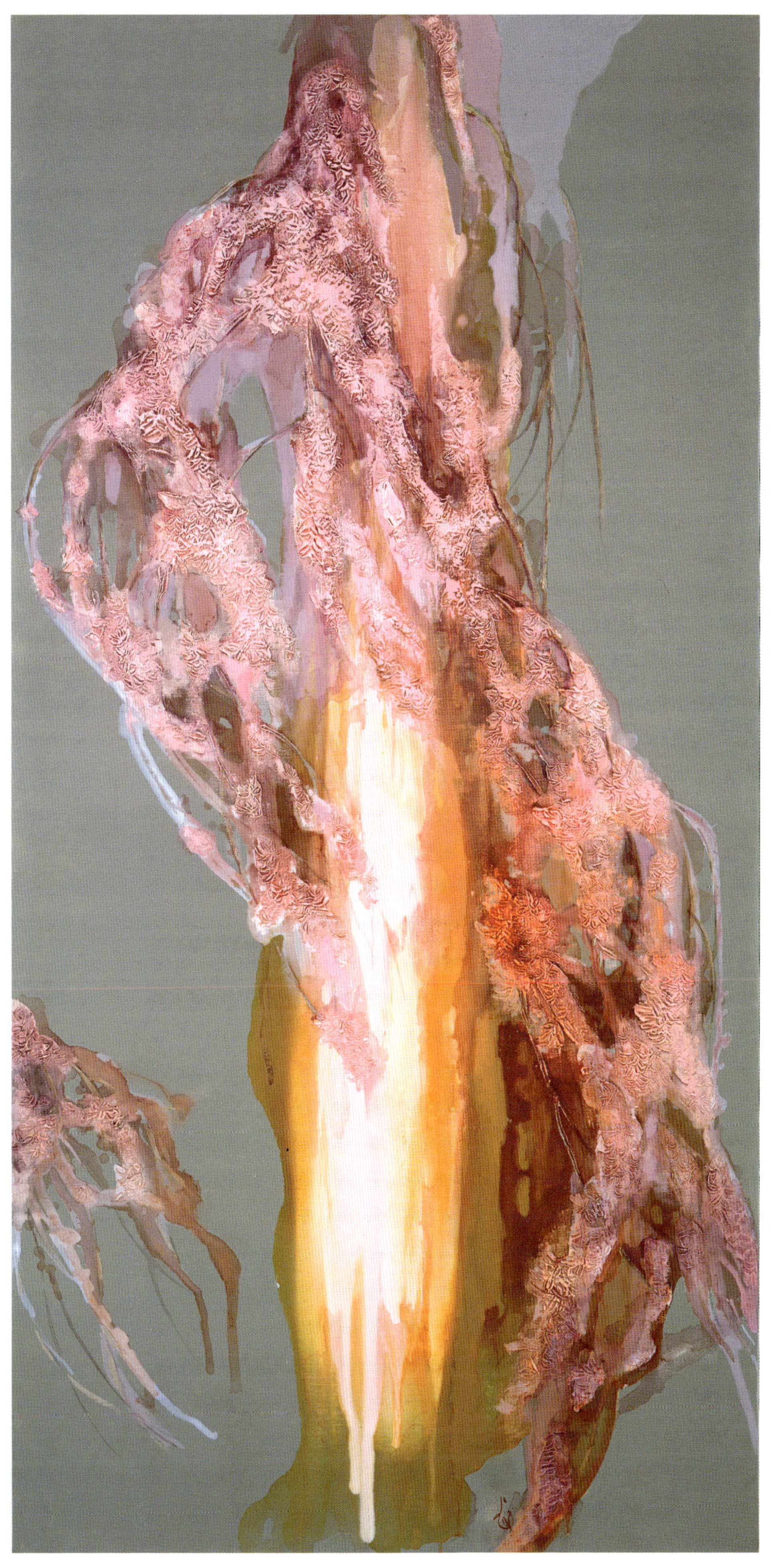

6

Spring (Floral Streamer)

1984. Oil on canvas. 78 3/4 × 39 3/8 inches. 200 × 100 cm.

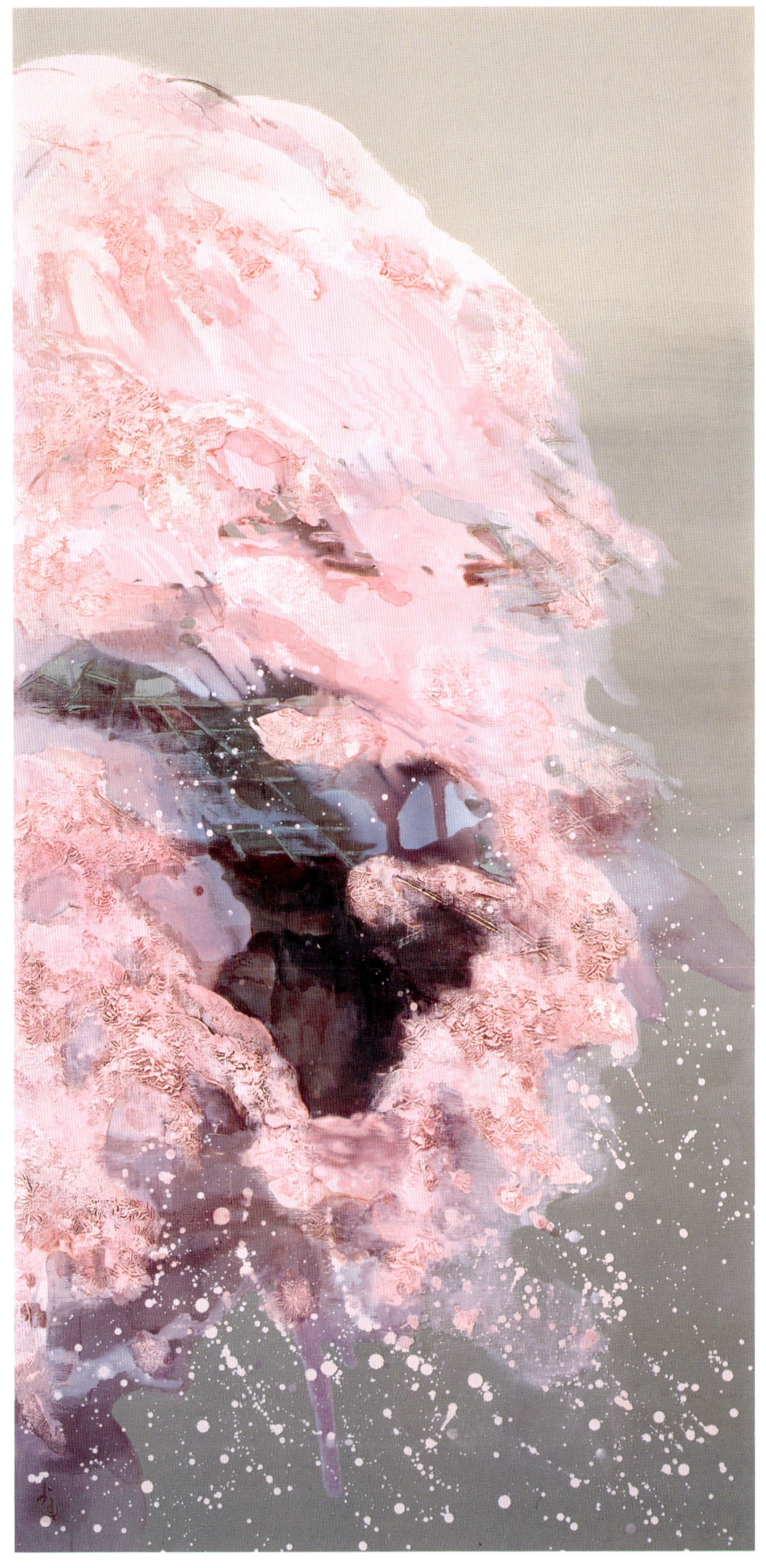

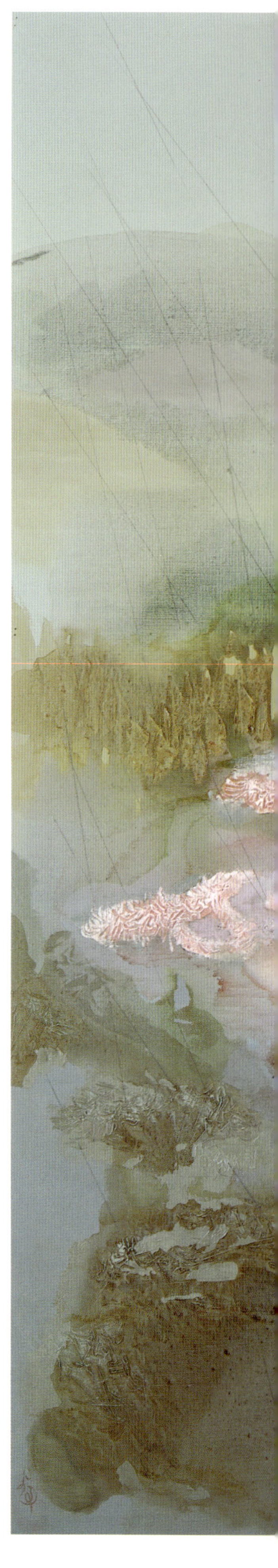

7
Rain (Mt. Yoshino)
1984. Oil on canvas. 70 7/8 × 70 7/8 inches. 180 × 180 cm.

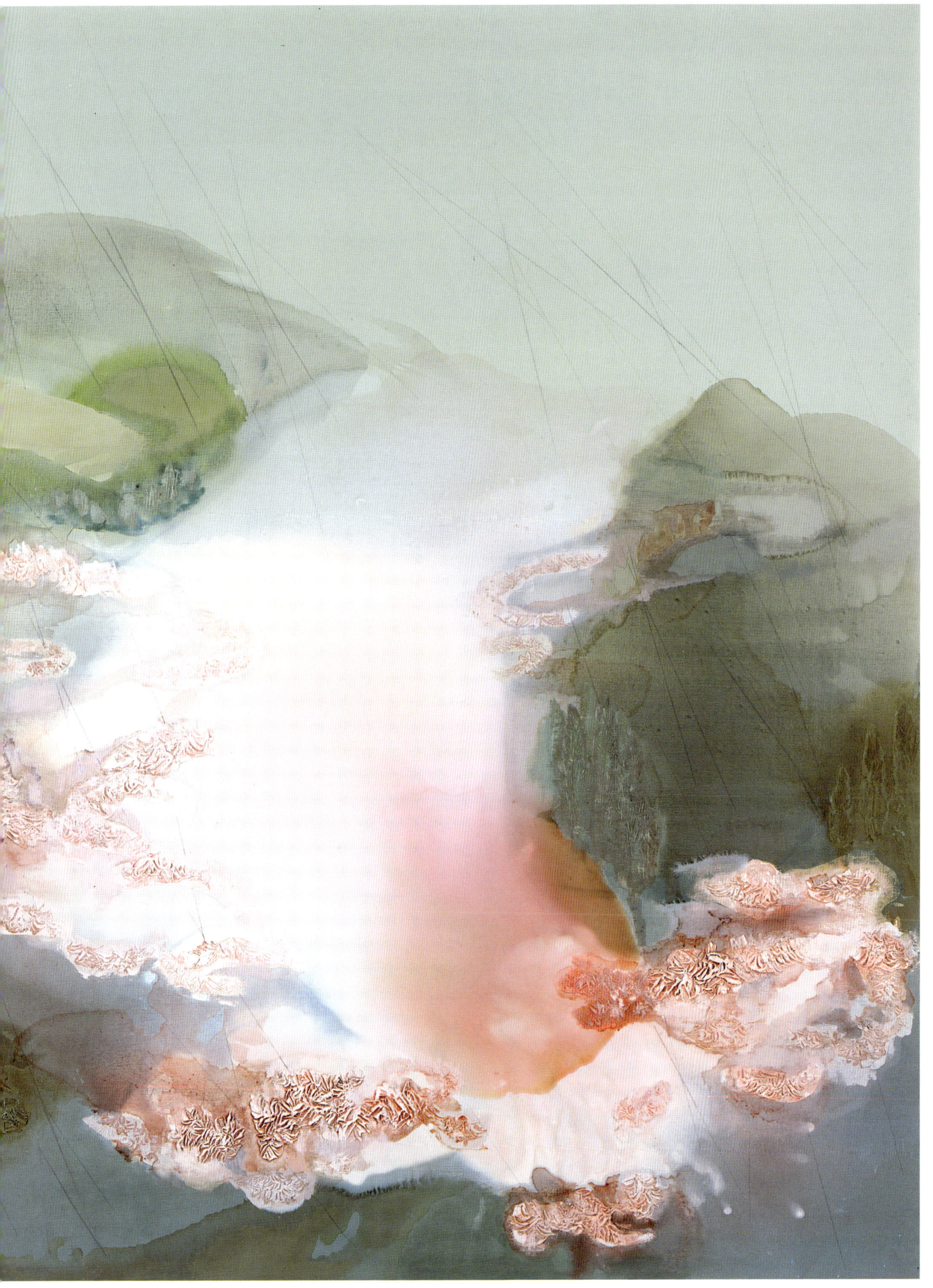

8

Cherry Blossoms at Twilight

1988. Oil on canvas. 59 1/8 × 31 1/2 inches. 150 × 80 cm.

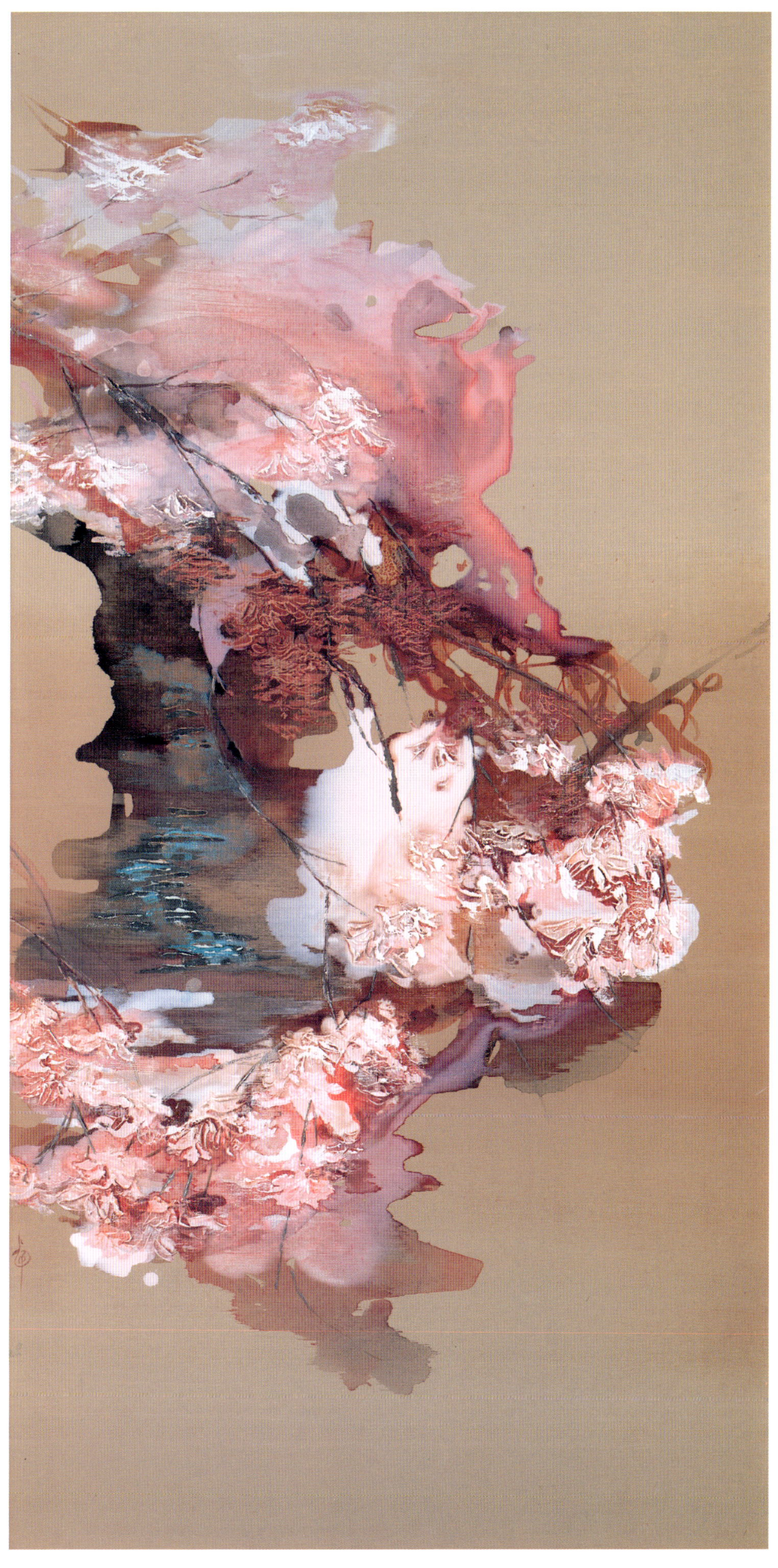

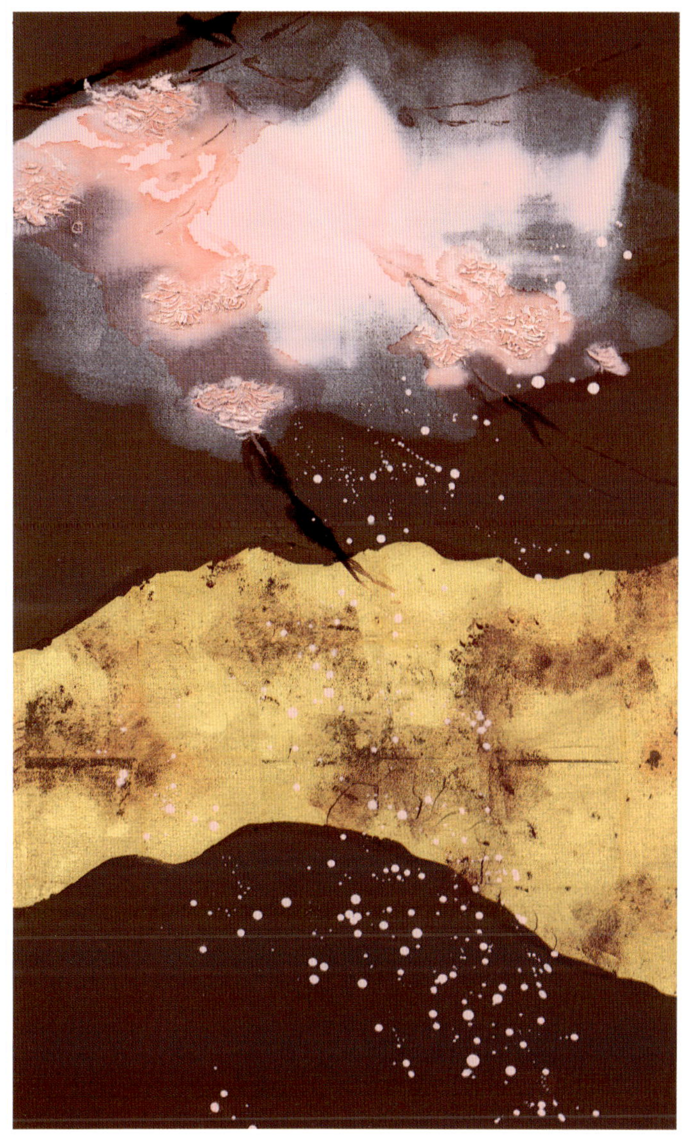

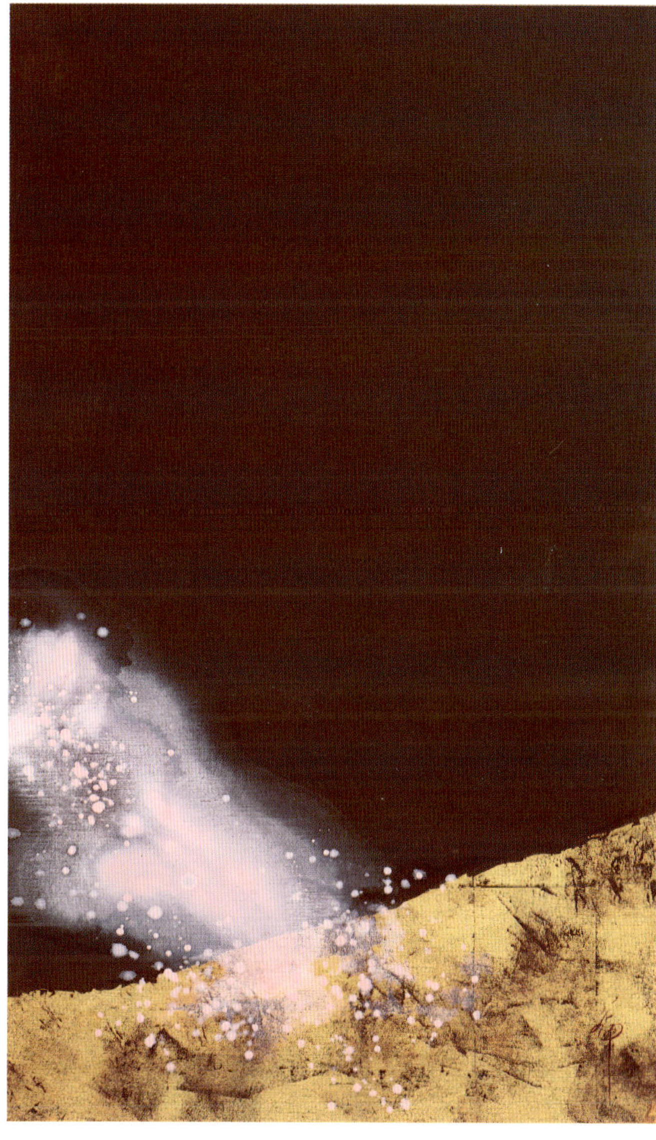

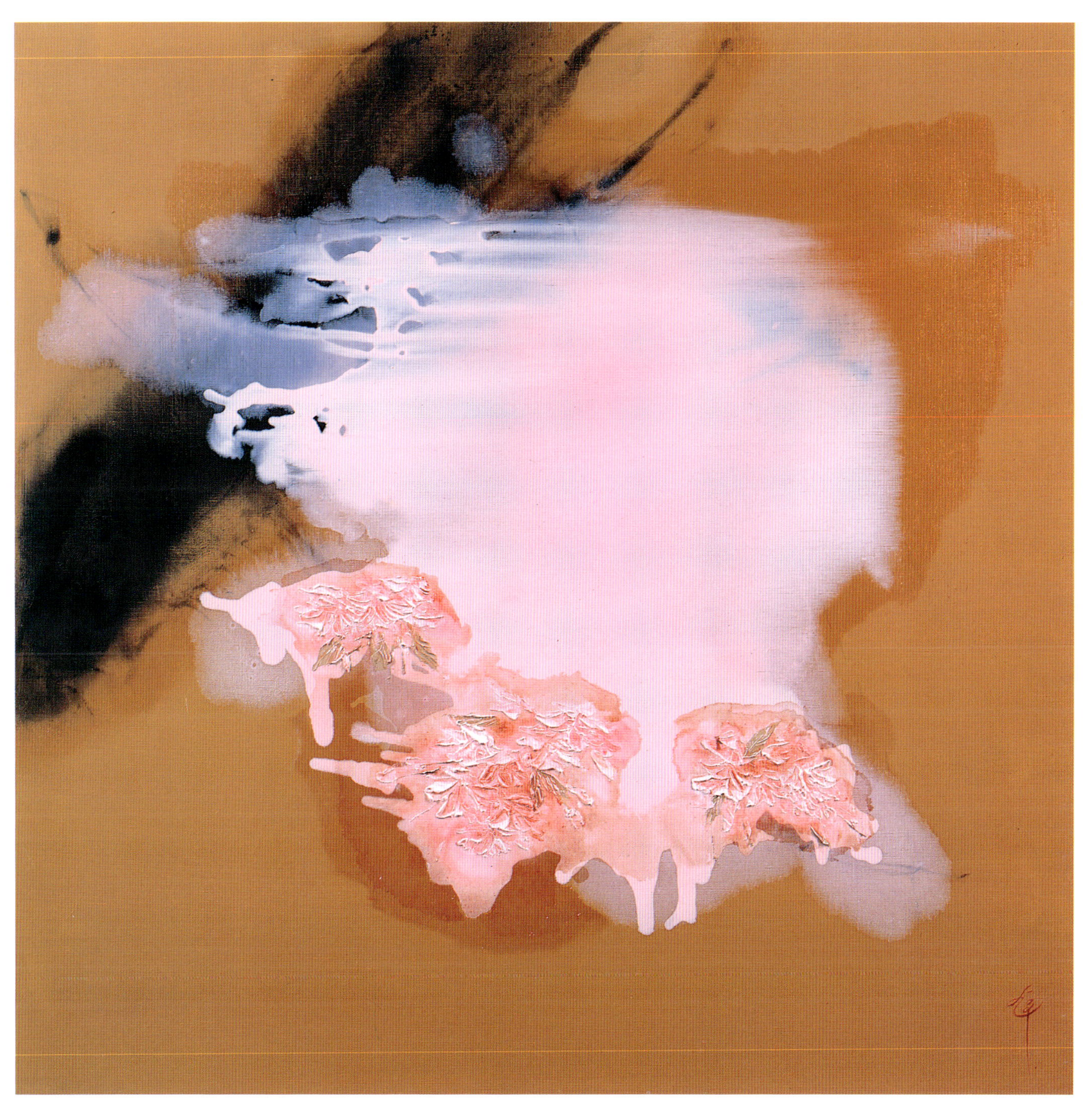

10
Double Cherry Blossoms (Fugenzo)
1992. Oil on canvas. 39 3/8 × 39 3/8 inches. 100 × 100 cm.

11

Flurry of Blossoms

1982. Oil on canvas. 39 3/8 × 23 5/8 inches. 100 × 60 cm.

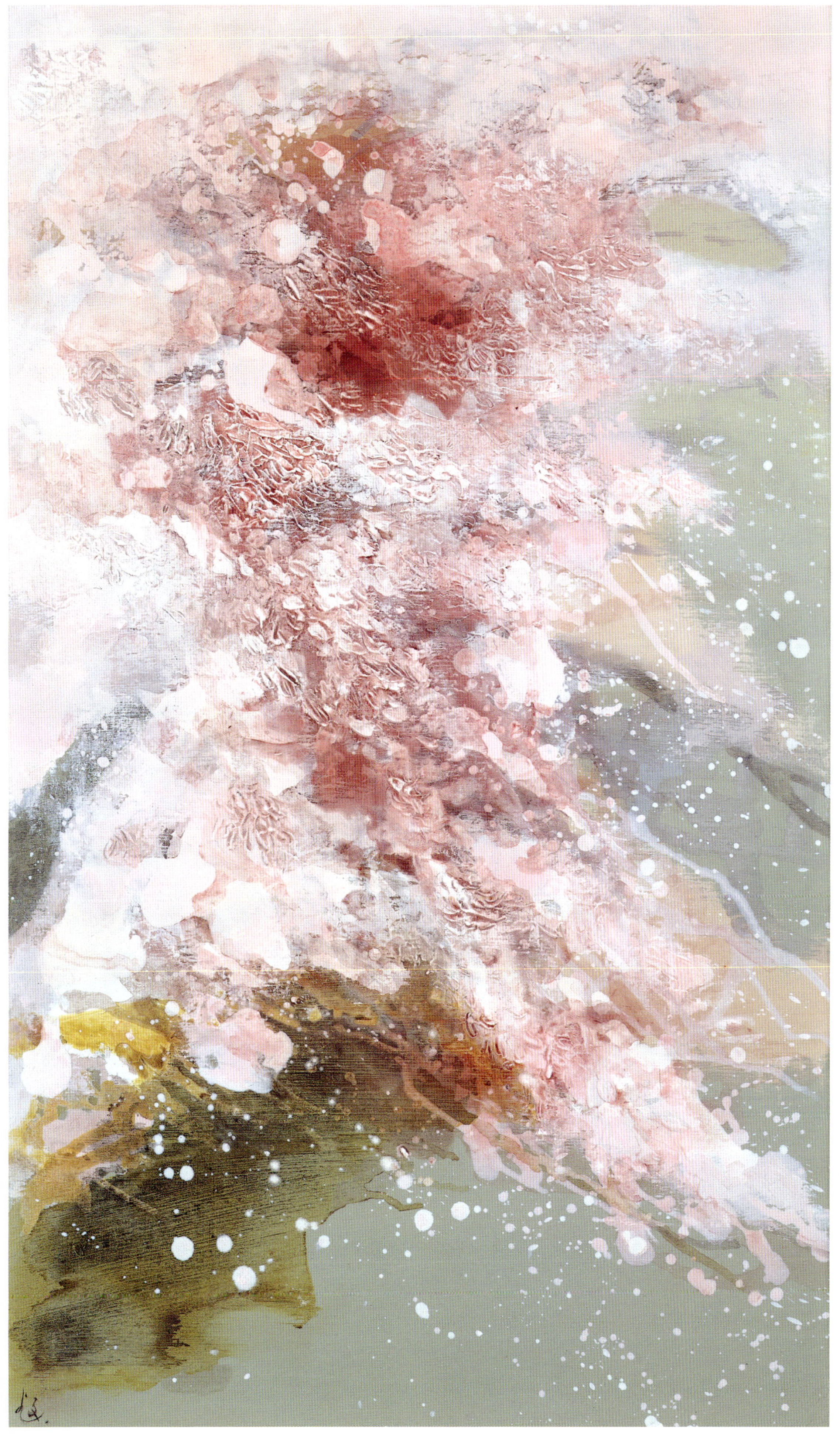

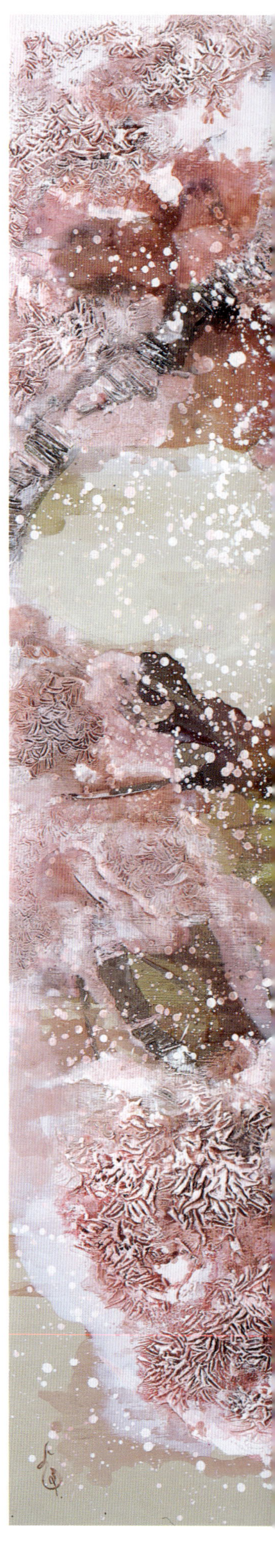

12
Wind (Flurry of Cherry Blossoms)
1984. Oil on canvas. $70\,7/8 \times 70\,7/8$ inches. 180×180 cm.

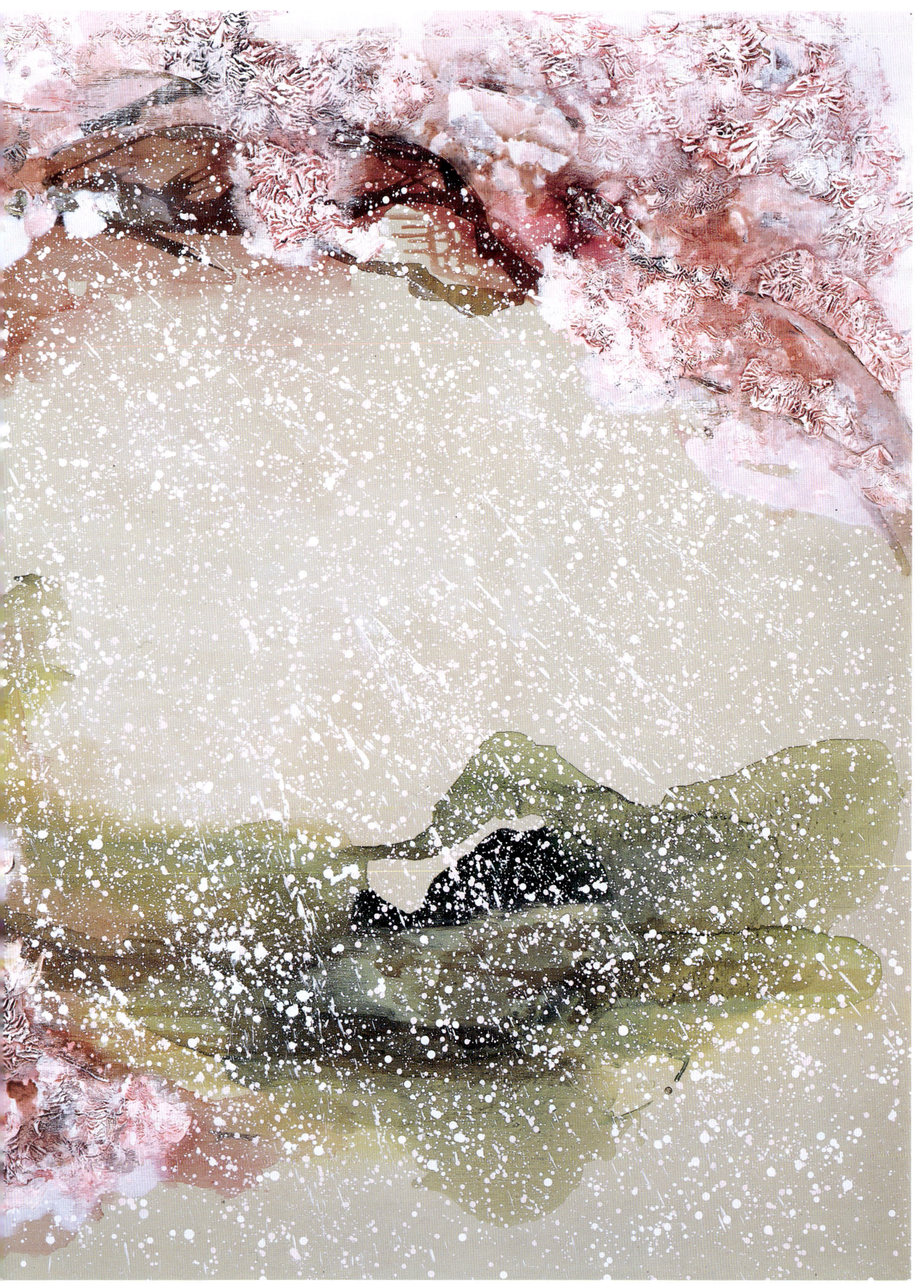

13

Flowery Clusters

1988. Oil on canvas. 59 1/8 × 31 1/2 inches. 150 × 80 cm.

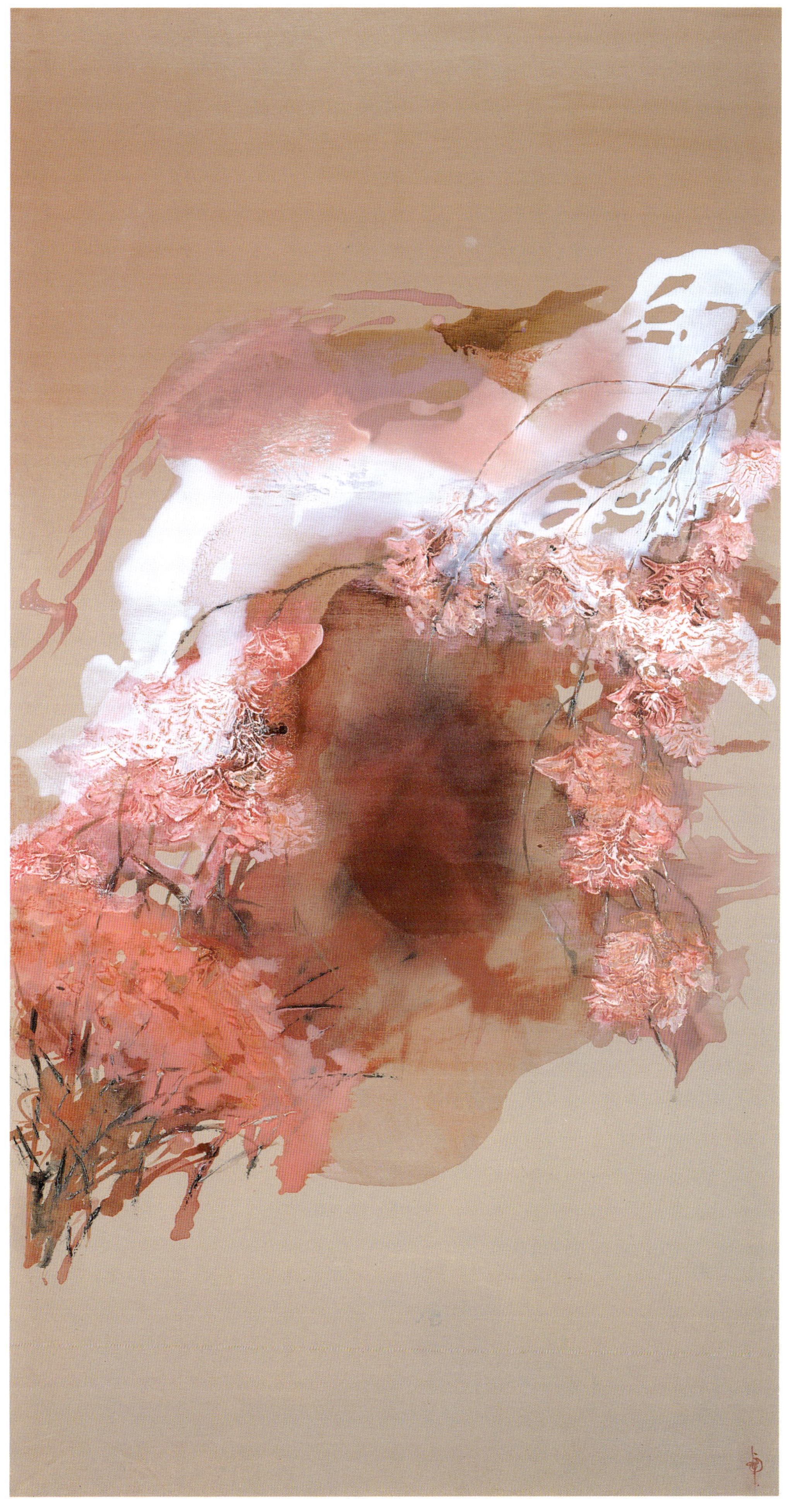

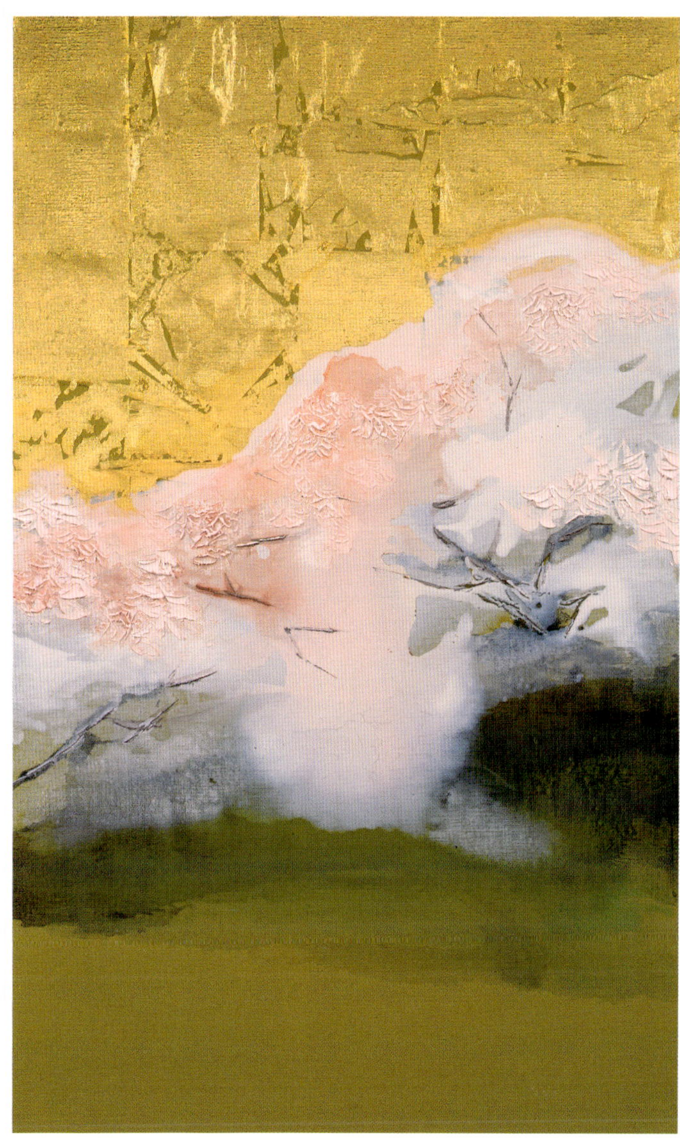
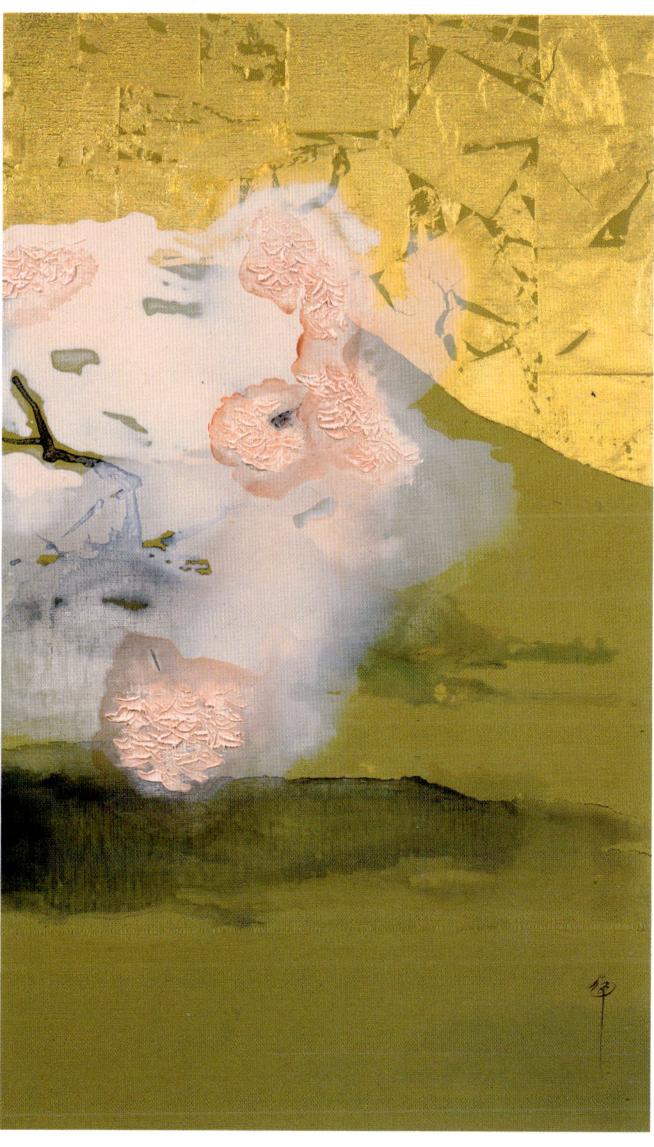

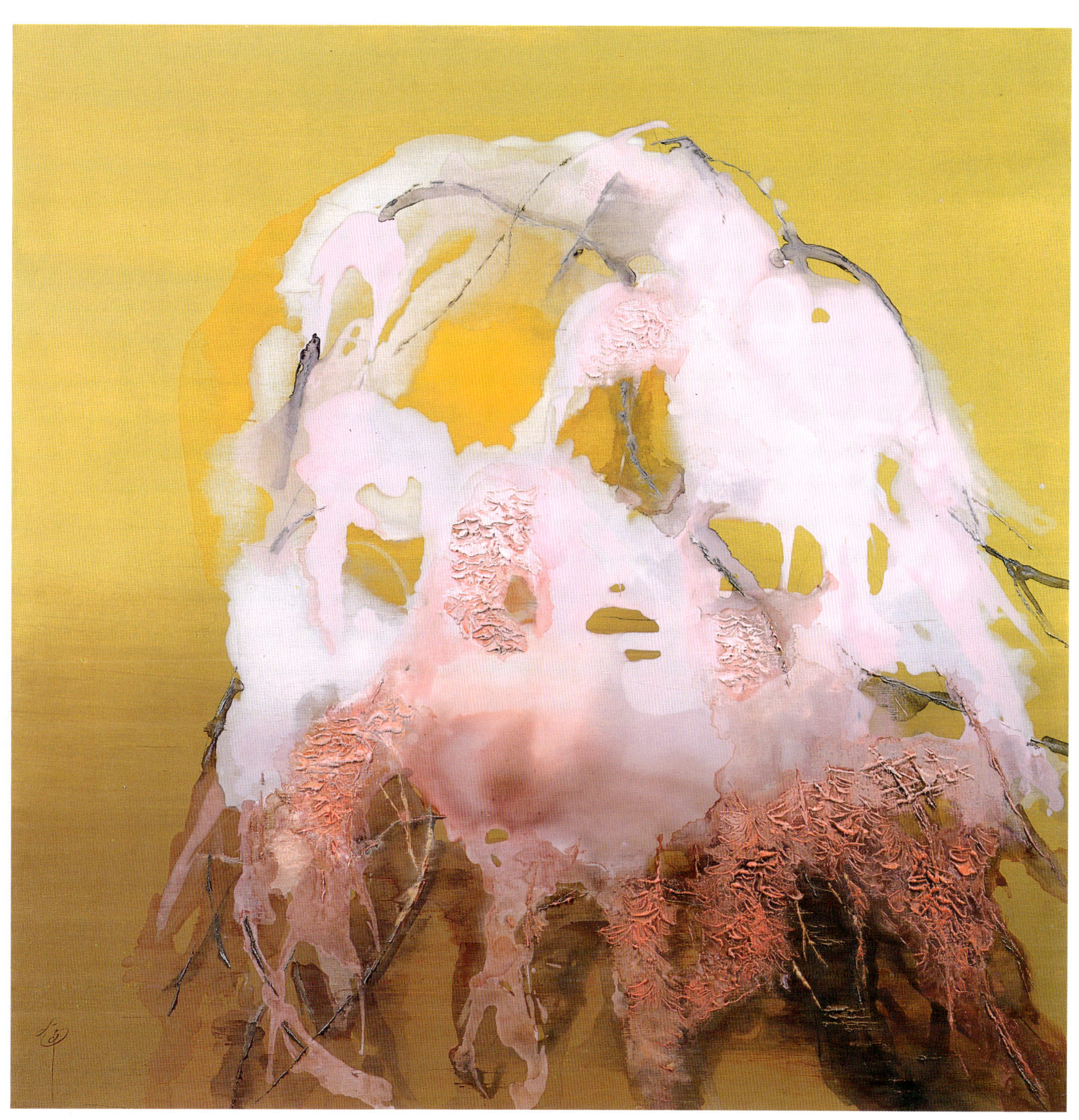

15

Evening Sunglow

1992. Oil on canvas. $39\frac{3}{8} \times 39\frac{3}{8}$ inches. 100×100 cm.

16

Early Spring (Magnolia)

1990. Oil on canvas. 59 1/8 × 31 1/2 inches. 150 × 80 cm.

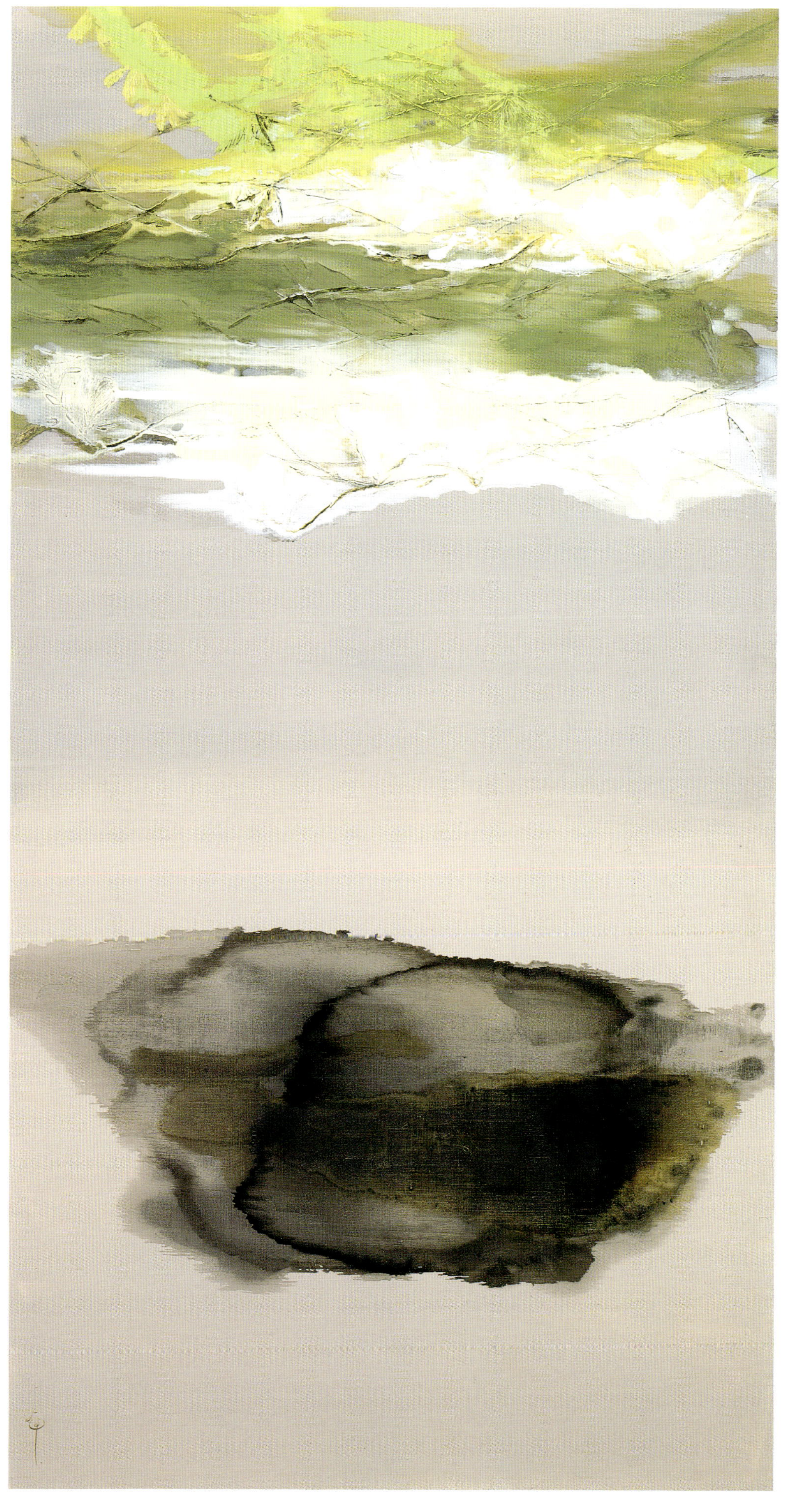

17

Early Spring (Fern)

1990. Oil on canvas. 59 1/8 × 31 1/2 inches. 150 × 80 cm.

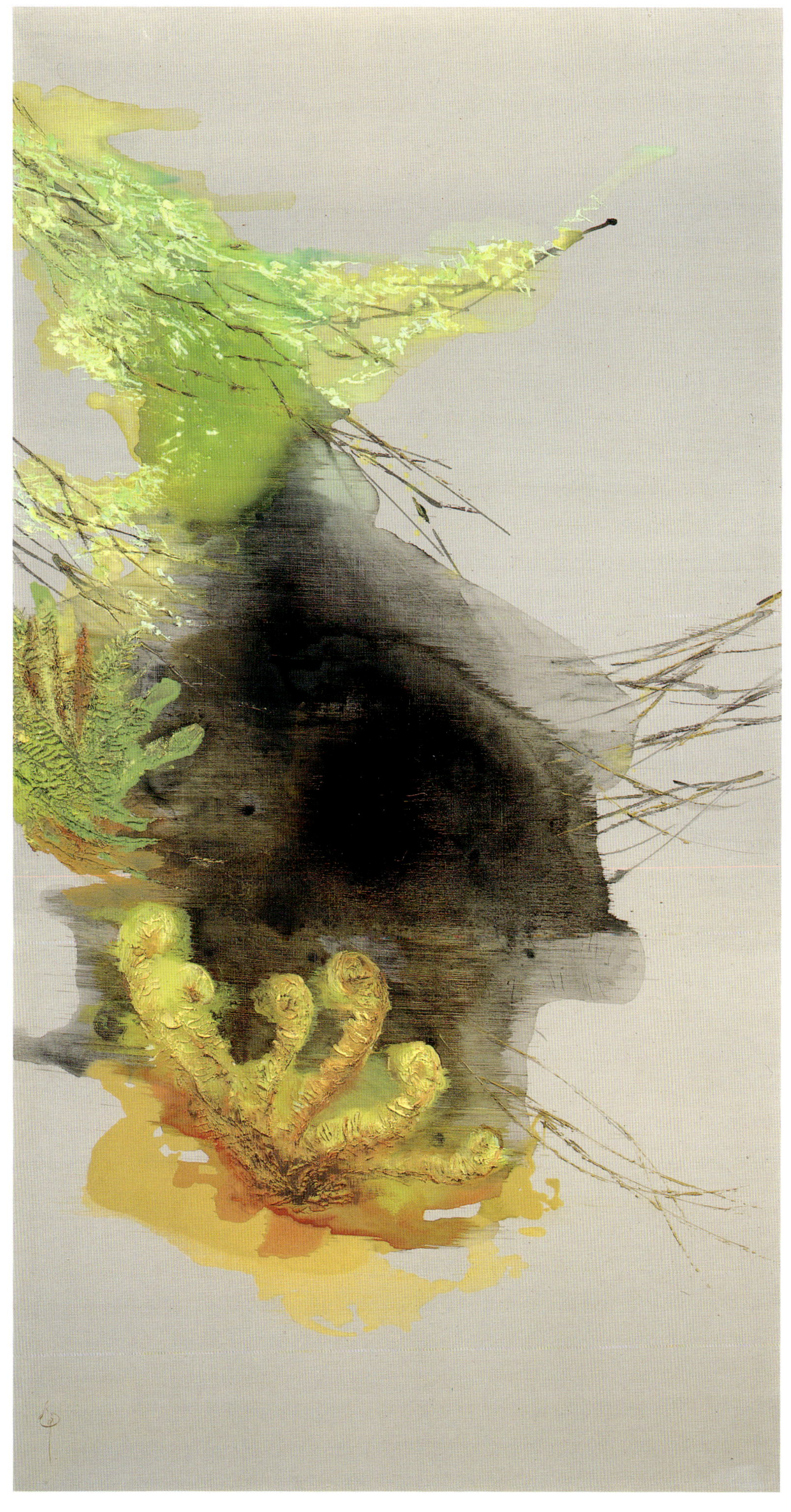

18

After Rain

1990. Oil on canvas. 59 1/8 × 27 1/2 inches. 150 × 70 cm.

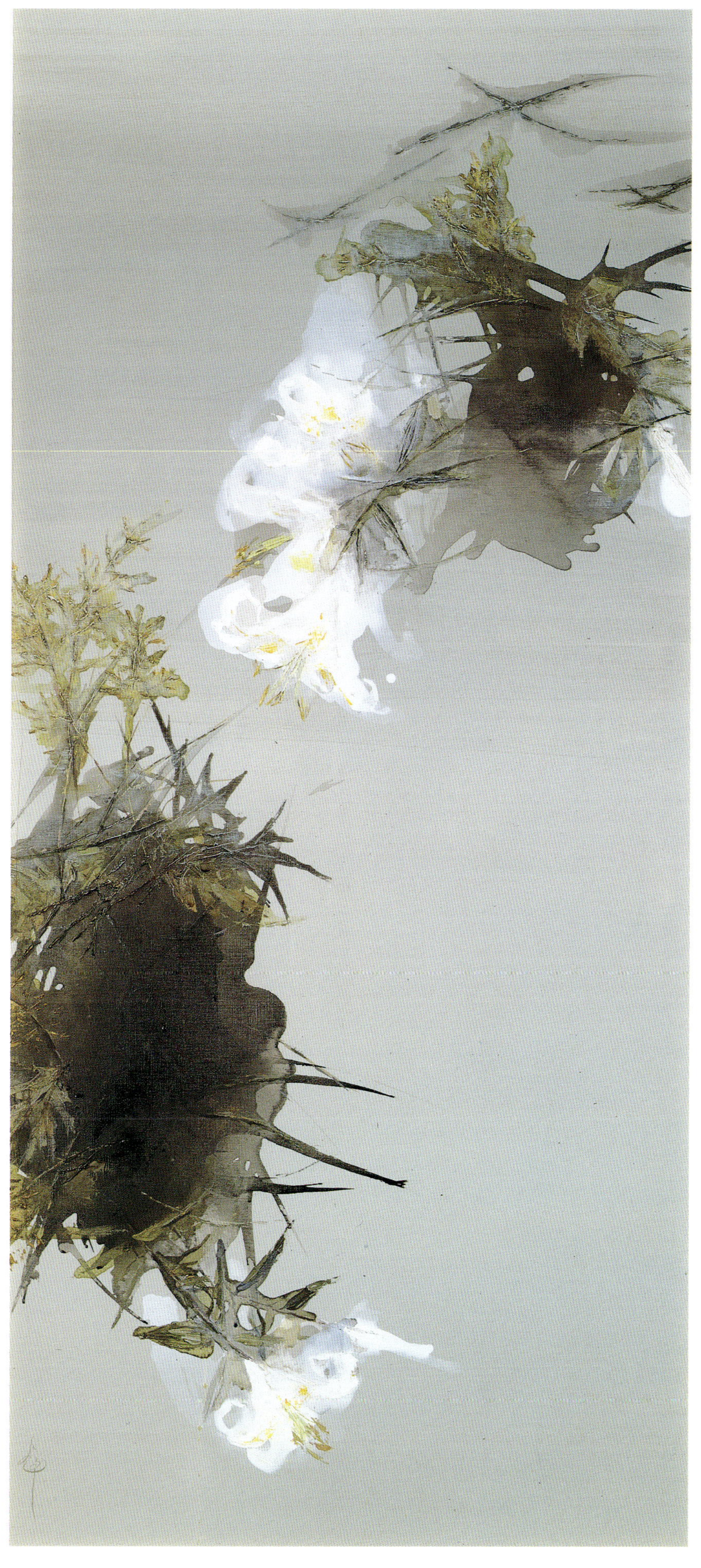

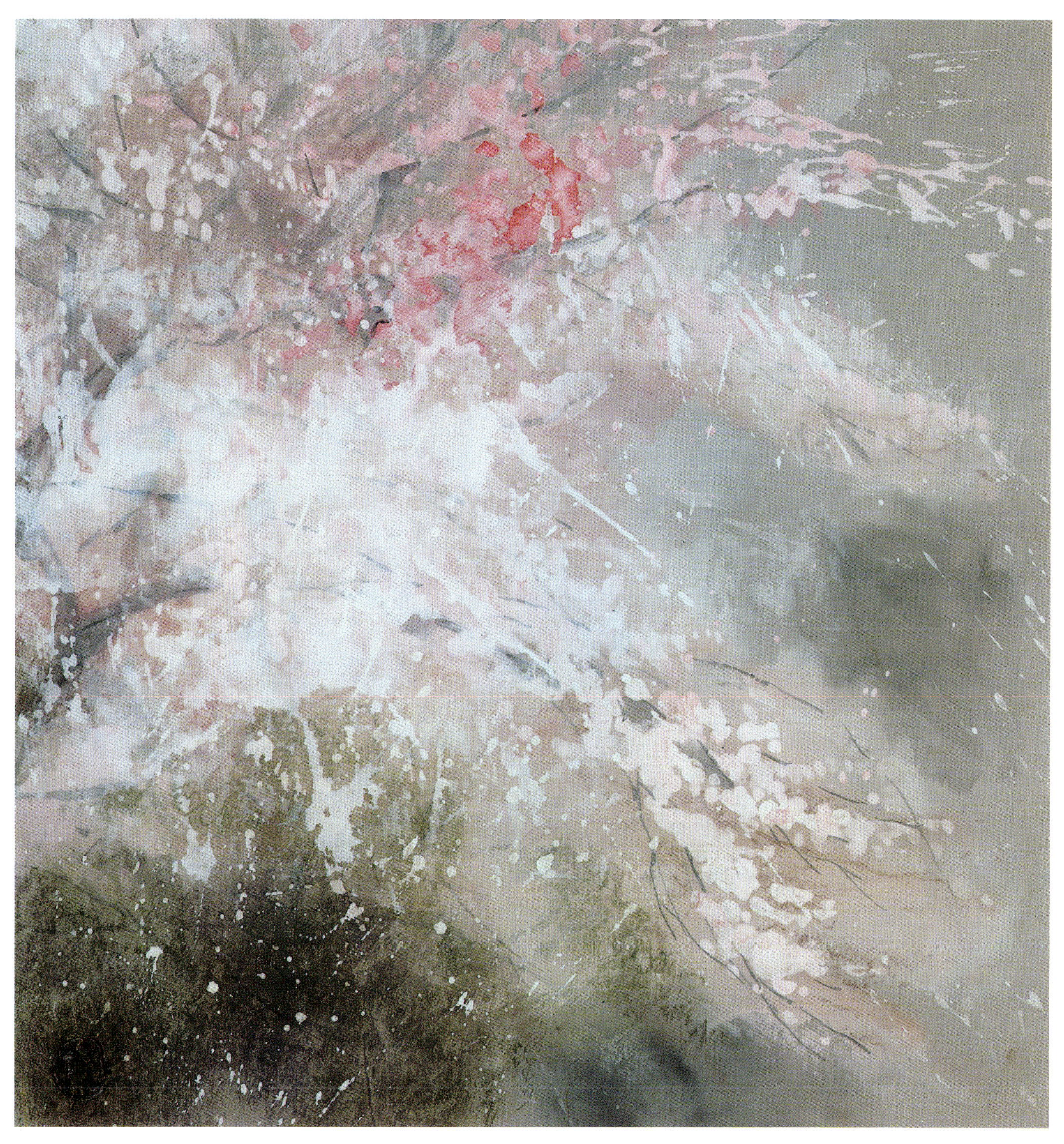

19

Flurry of Blossoms

1980. Pastel, gouache and Chinese ink on paper. $20\,1/8 \times 19\,1/4$ inches. 51×49 cm.

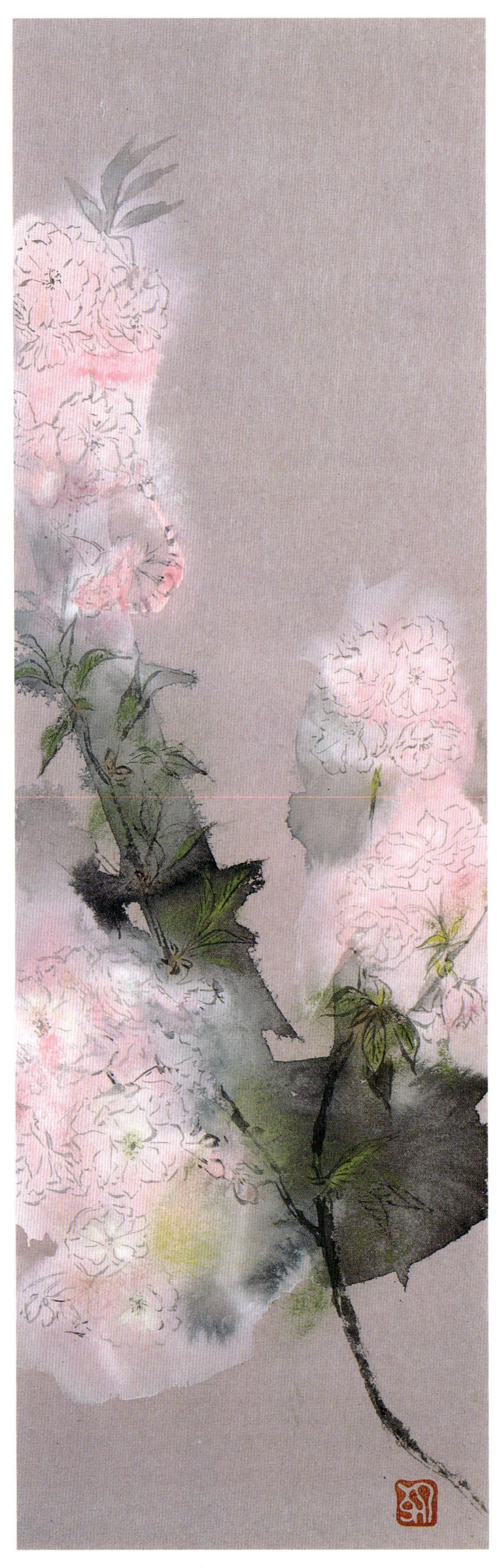

20
Double Cherry Blossoms (A)
1992. Pastel, gouache and Chinese ink on paper. 25 3/8 × 8 1/8 inches. 64.5 × 20.5 cm.

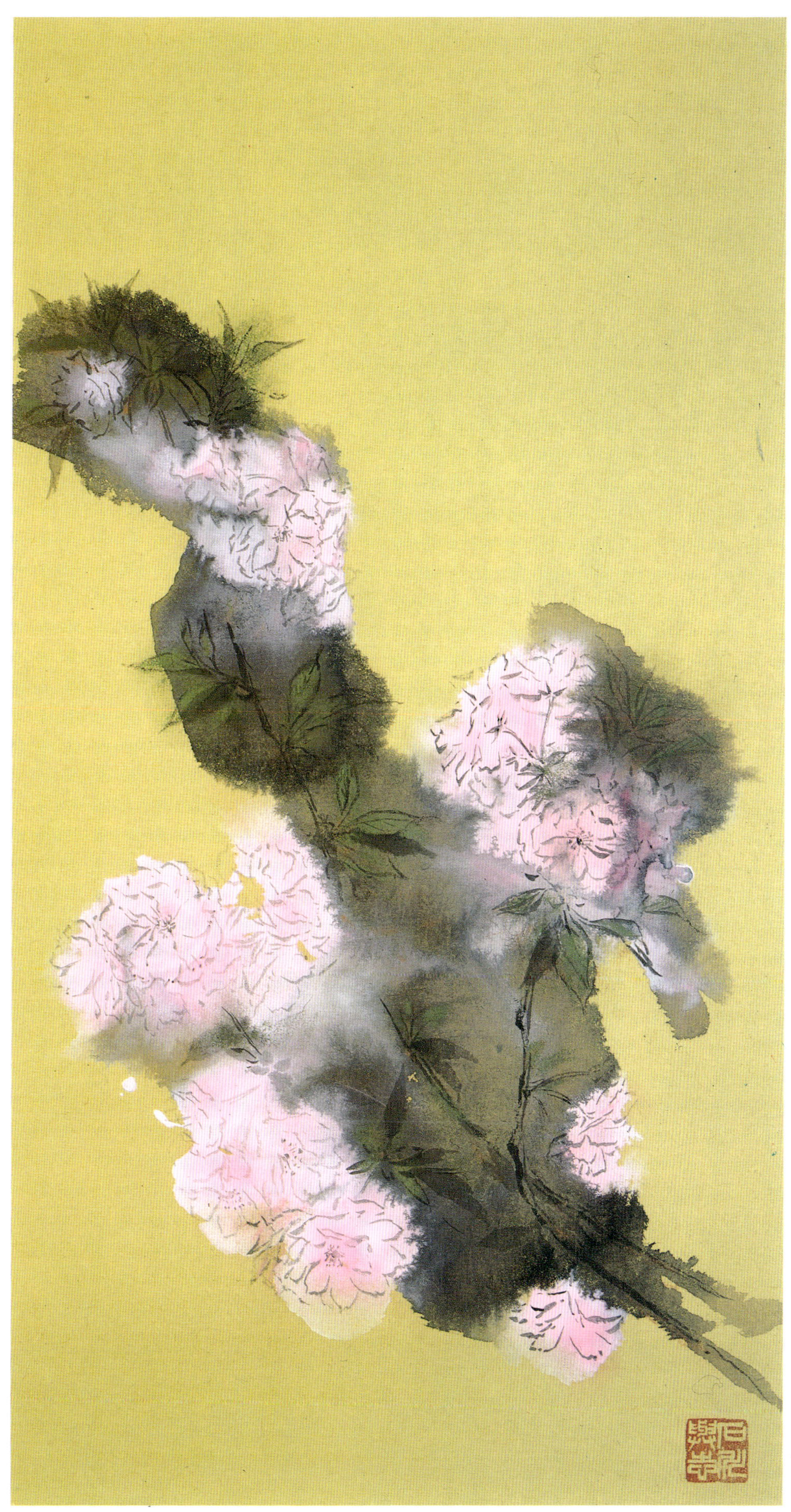

21
Double Cherry Blossoms (B)
1992. Pastel, gouache and Chinese ink on paper. 25 × 13 1/2 inches. 63.5 × 34.5 cm.

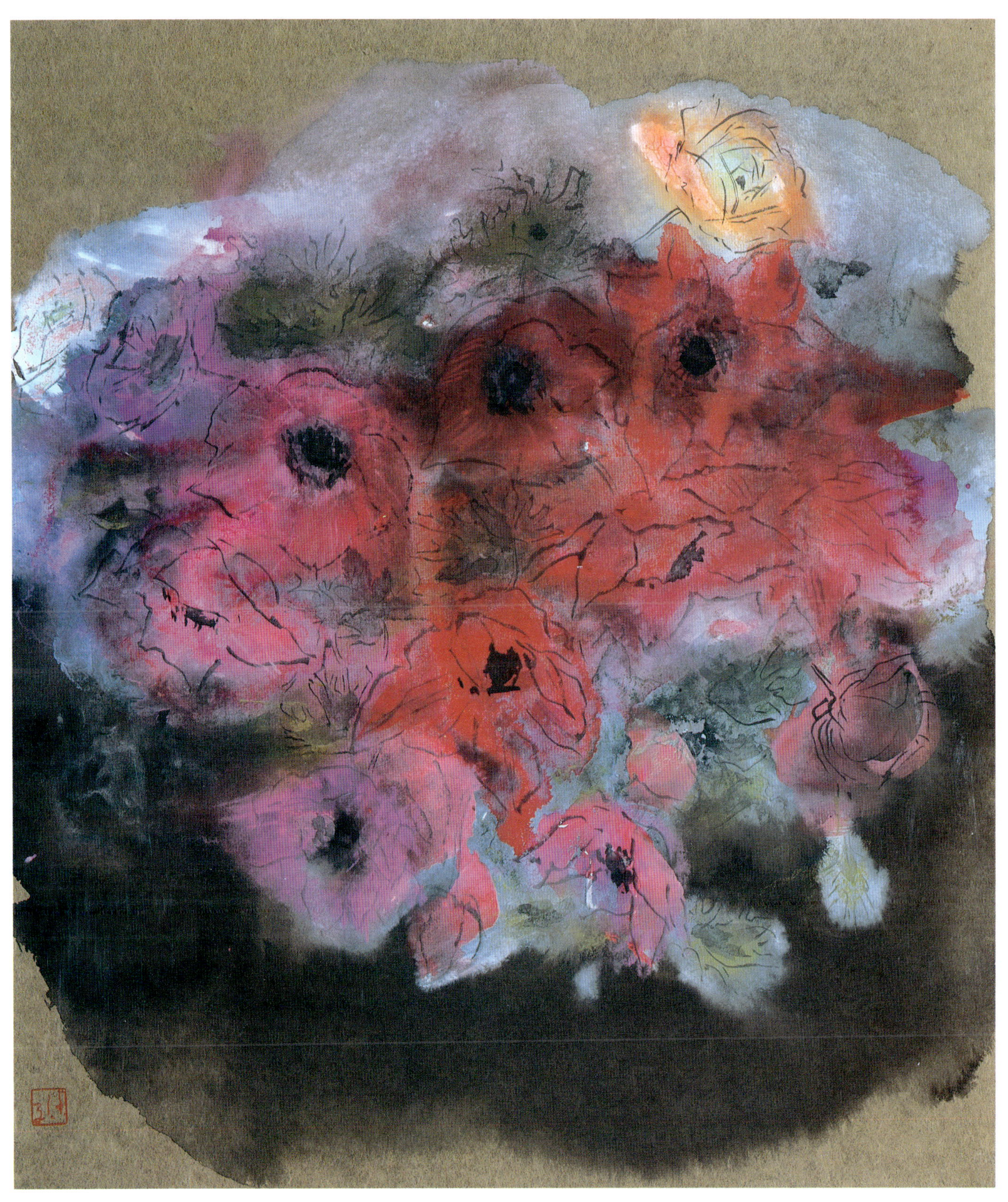

22
Anemone
1984. Pastel, gouache and Chinese ink on paper. 20 1/8 × 17 1/4 inches. 51 × 44 cm.

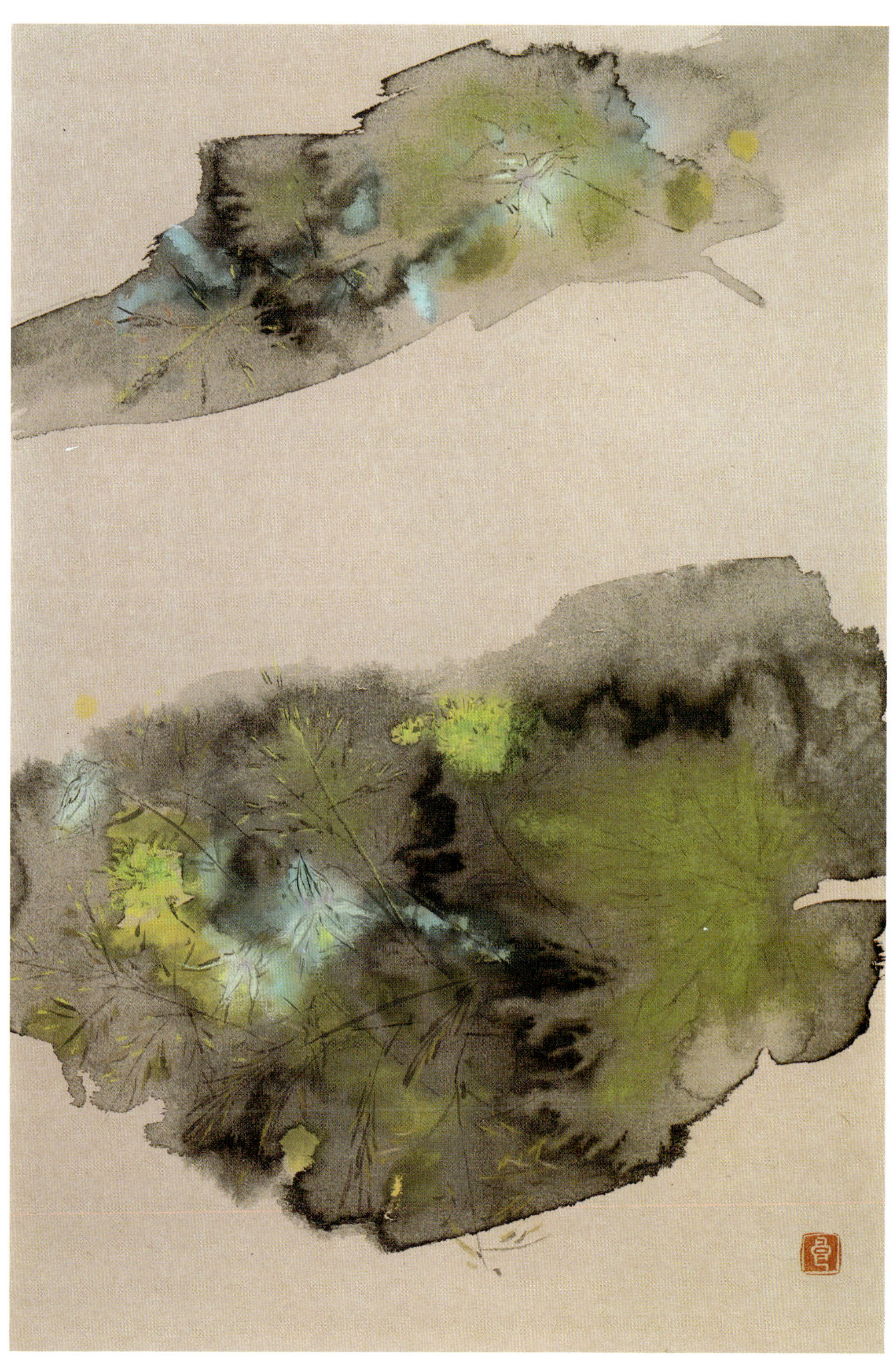

23
Columbine
1990. Pastel, gouache and Chinese ink on paper. 18 1/2 × 12 5/8 inches. 47 × 32 cm.

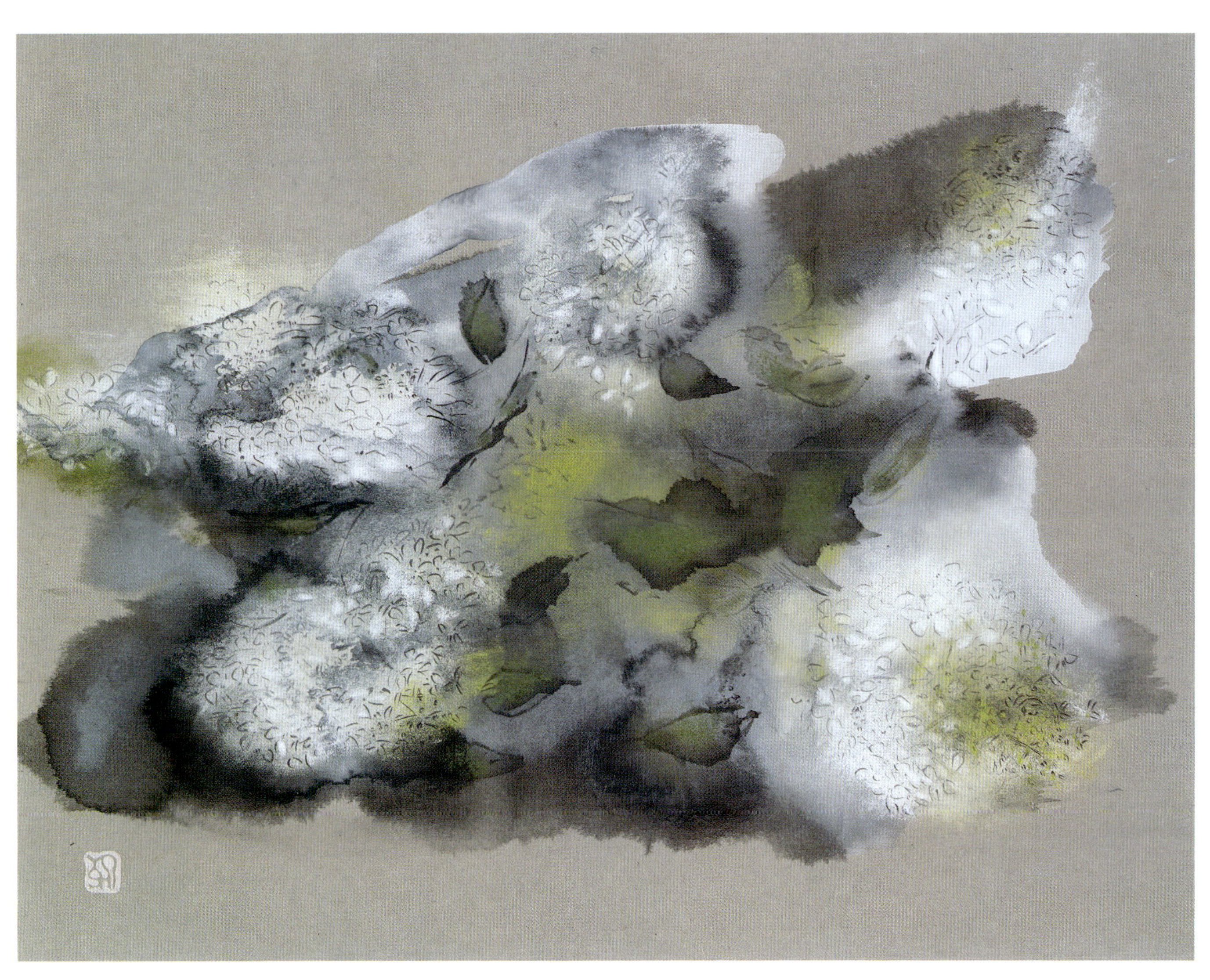

24

June Flowers

1984. Pastel, gouache and Chinese ink on paper. 18 1/8 × 23 5/8 inches. 46 × 60 cm.

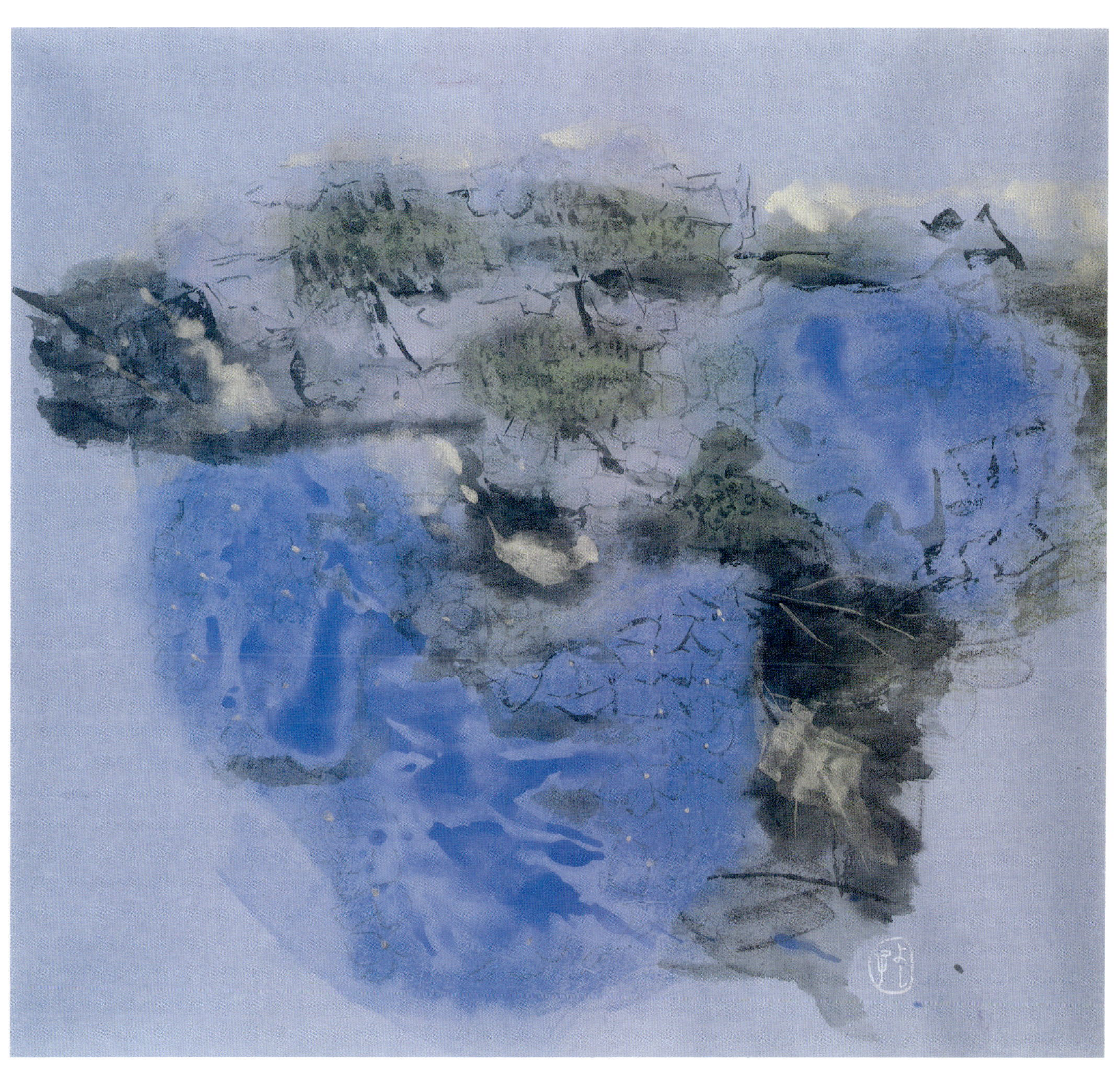

25
Hydrangea
1980. Pastel, gouache and Chinese ink on paper. $20\,1/2 \times 22\,1/4$ inches. 52×56.5 cm.

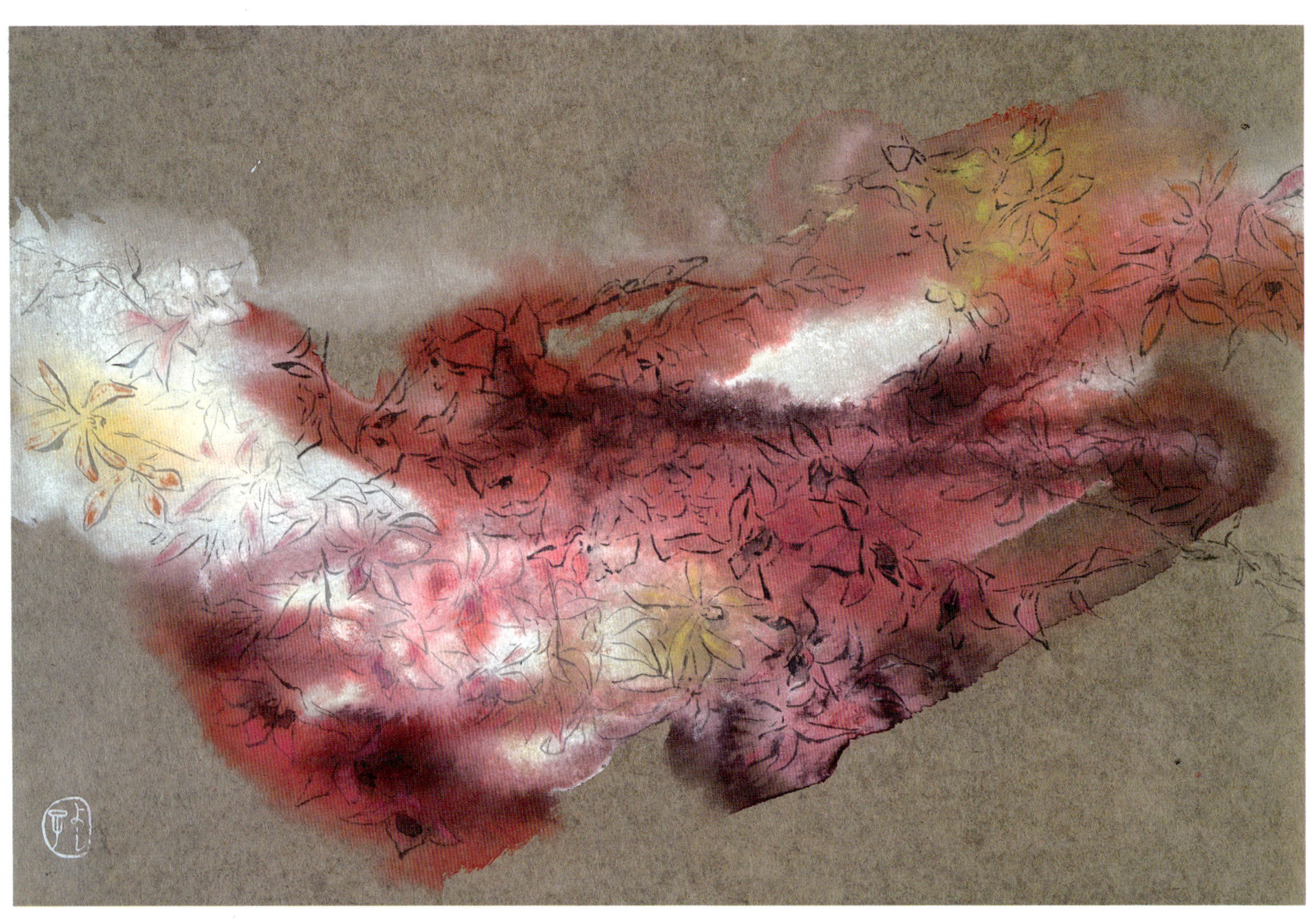

26

Orchid

1984. Pastel, gouache and Chinese ink on paper. $15\frac{3}{4} \times 23\frac{5}{8}$ inches. 40×60 cm.

27

Black Lily

1984. Pastel, gouache and Chinese ink on paper. 12 1/4 × 18 1/8 inches. 31 × 46 cm.

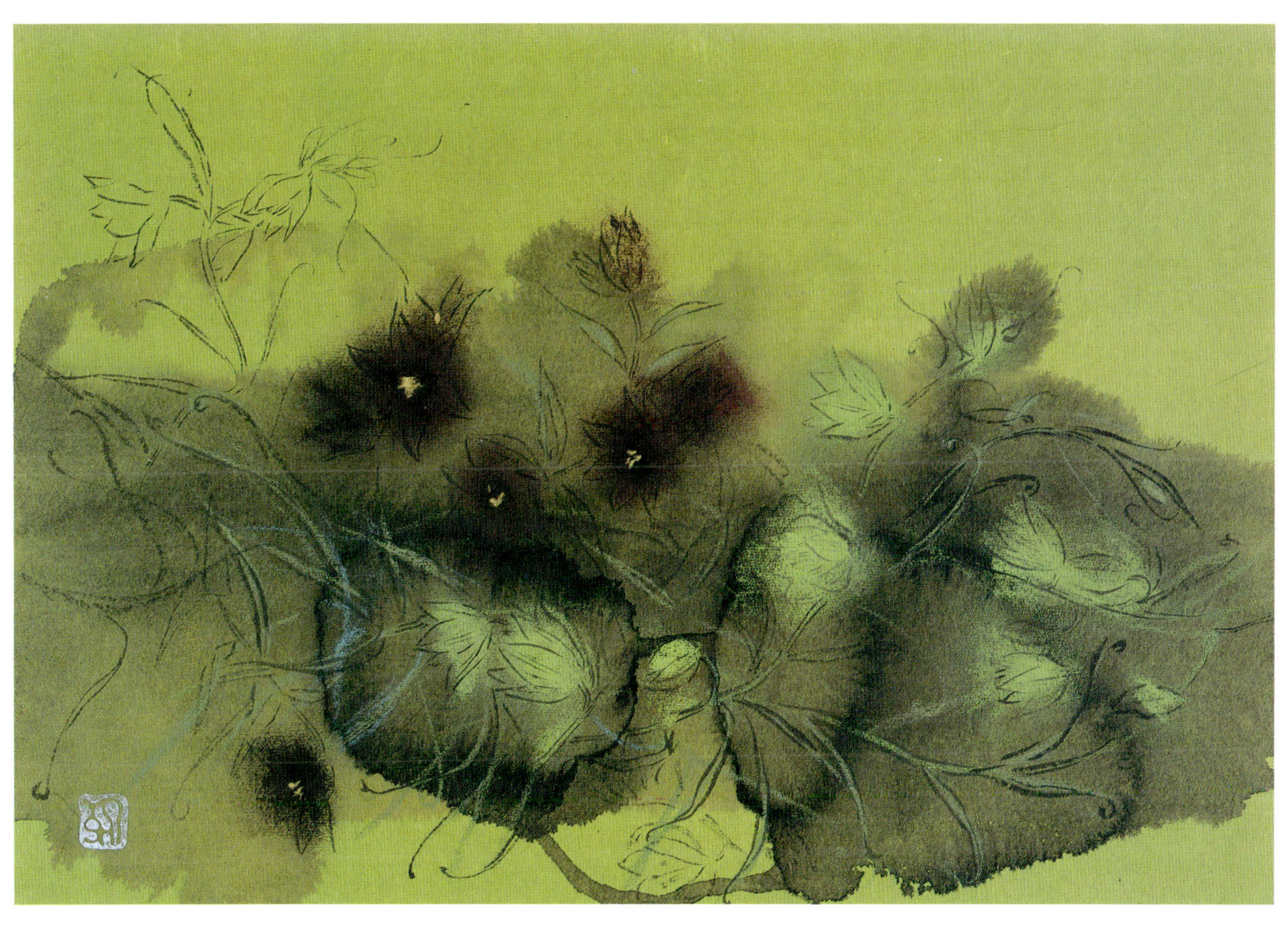

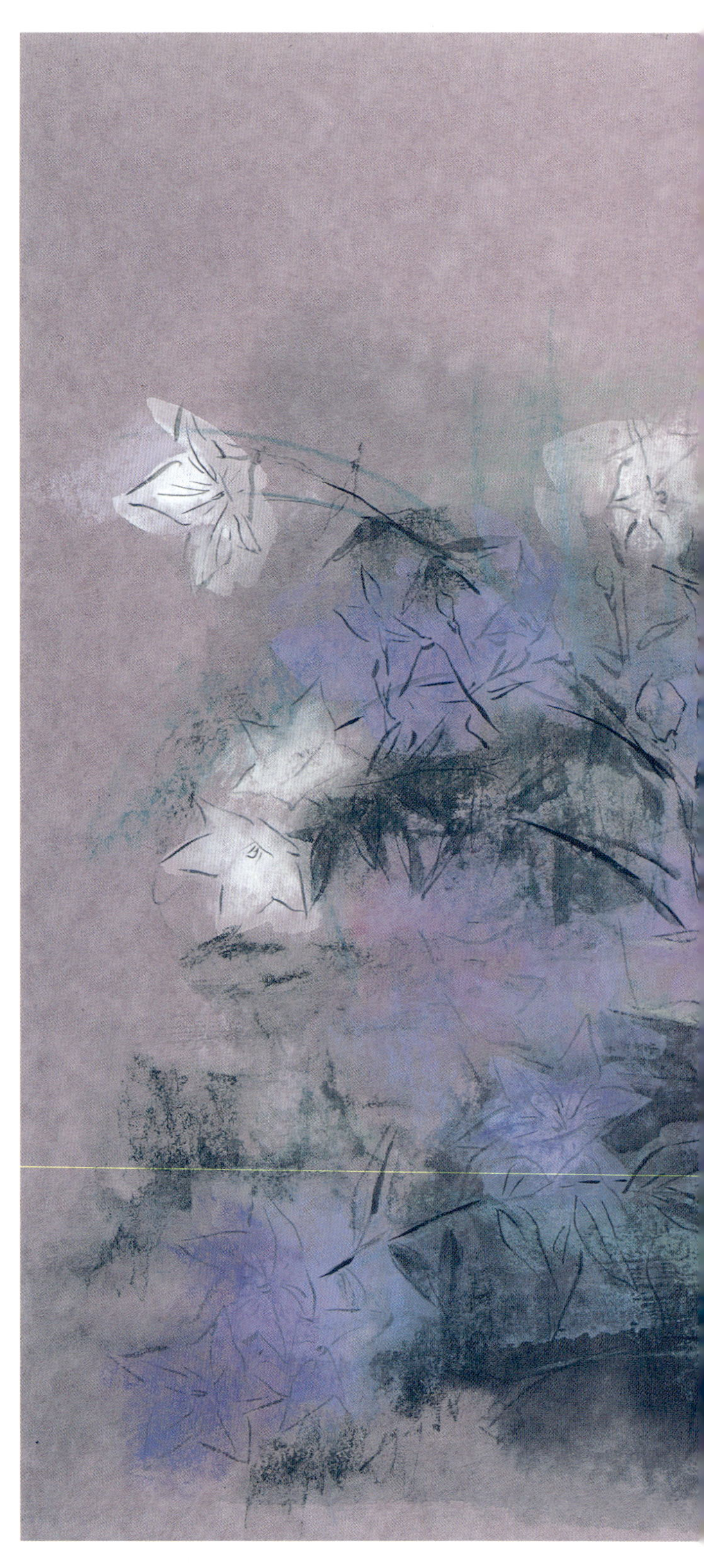

28

Chinese Bellflower

1978. Pastel, gouache and Chinese ink on paper. 21 1/8 × 30 3/4 inches. 53.5 × 78 cm.

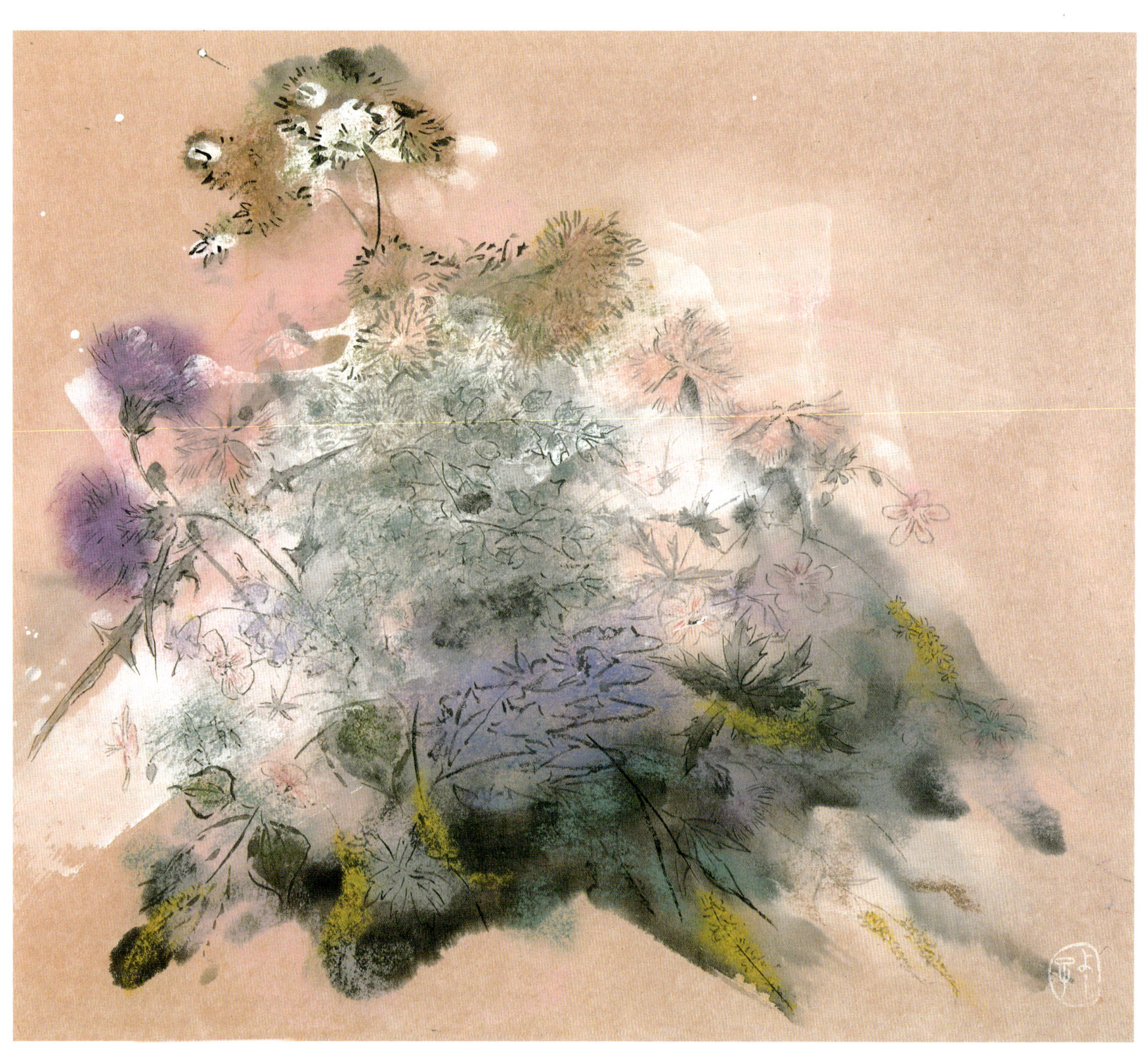

29

Alpine Flowers

1979. Pastel, gouache and Chinese ink on paper. 17 1/4 × 19 3/4 inches. 44 × 50 cm.

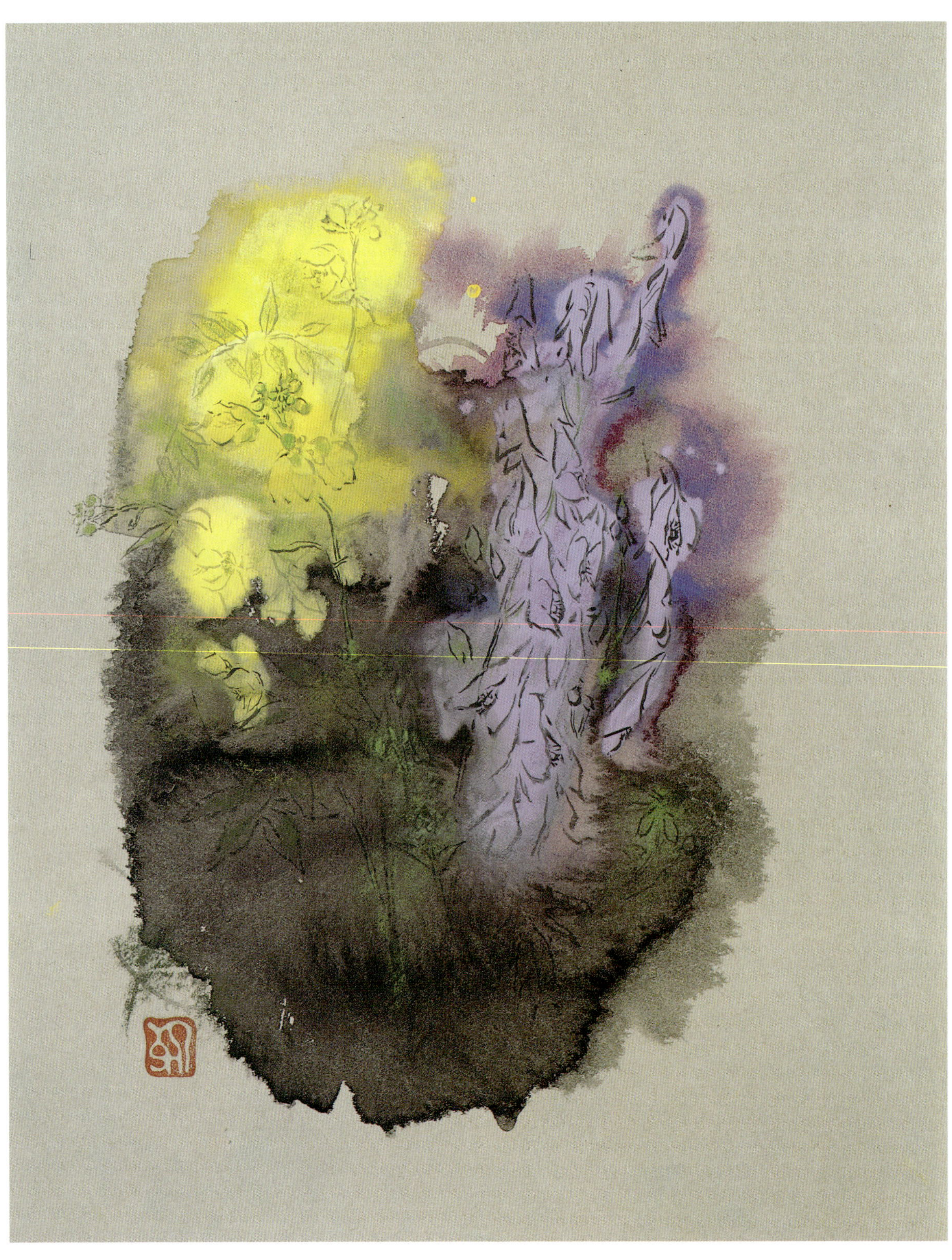

30

Aconite

1990. Pastel, gouache and Chinese ink on paper. 15 3/4 × 12 3/4 inches. 40 × 32.5 cm.

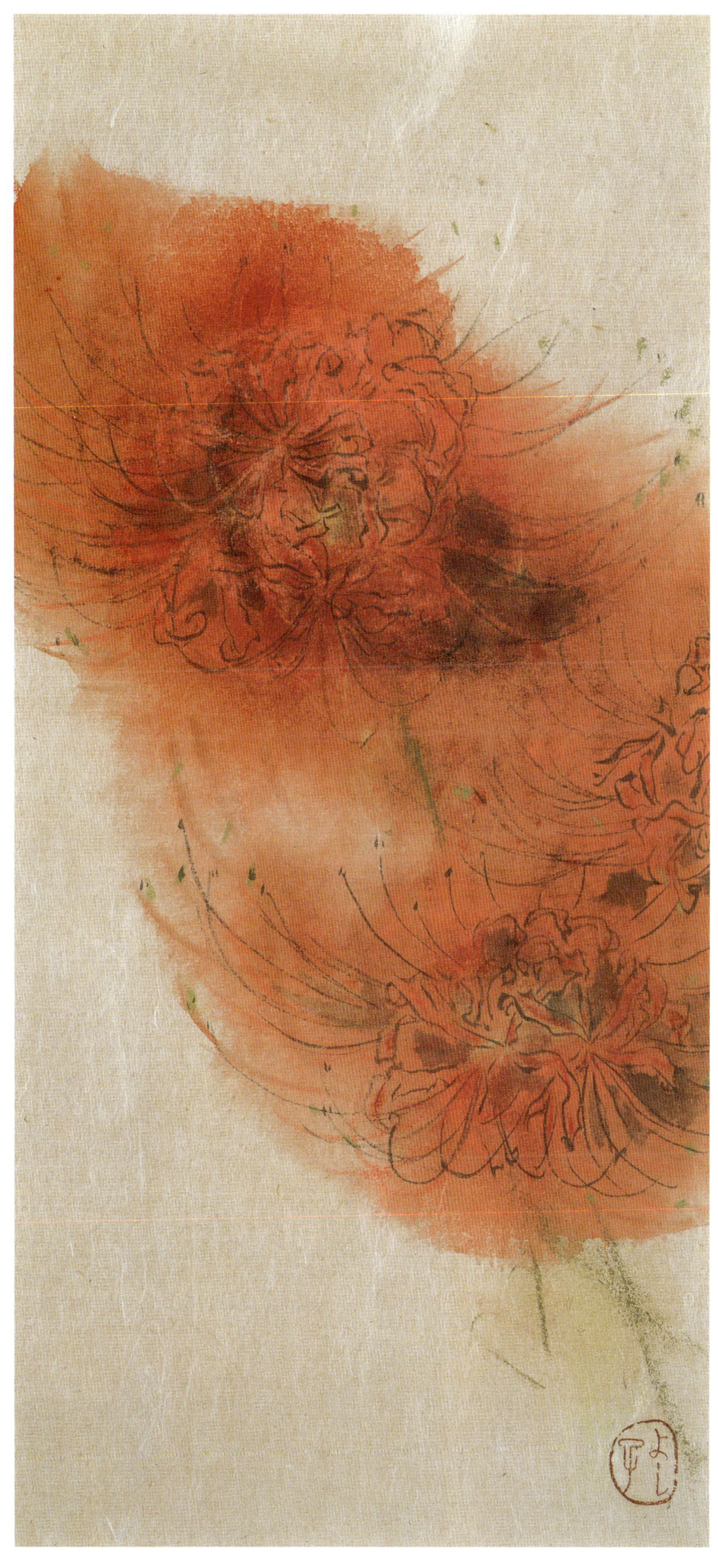

31

Amaryllis

1980. Pastel, gouache and Chinese ink on paper.
$19\,3/4 \times 9\,1/2$ inches. 50×24 cm.

32

Feminine Flowers

1990. Pastel, gouache and Chinese ink on paper. $18\frac{3}{4} \times 11$ inches. 47.5×28 cm.

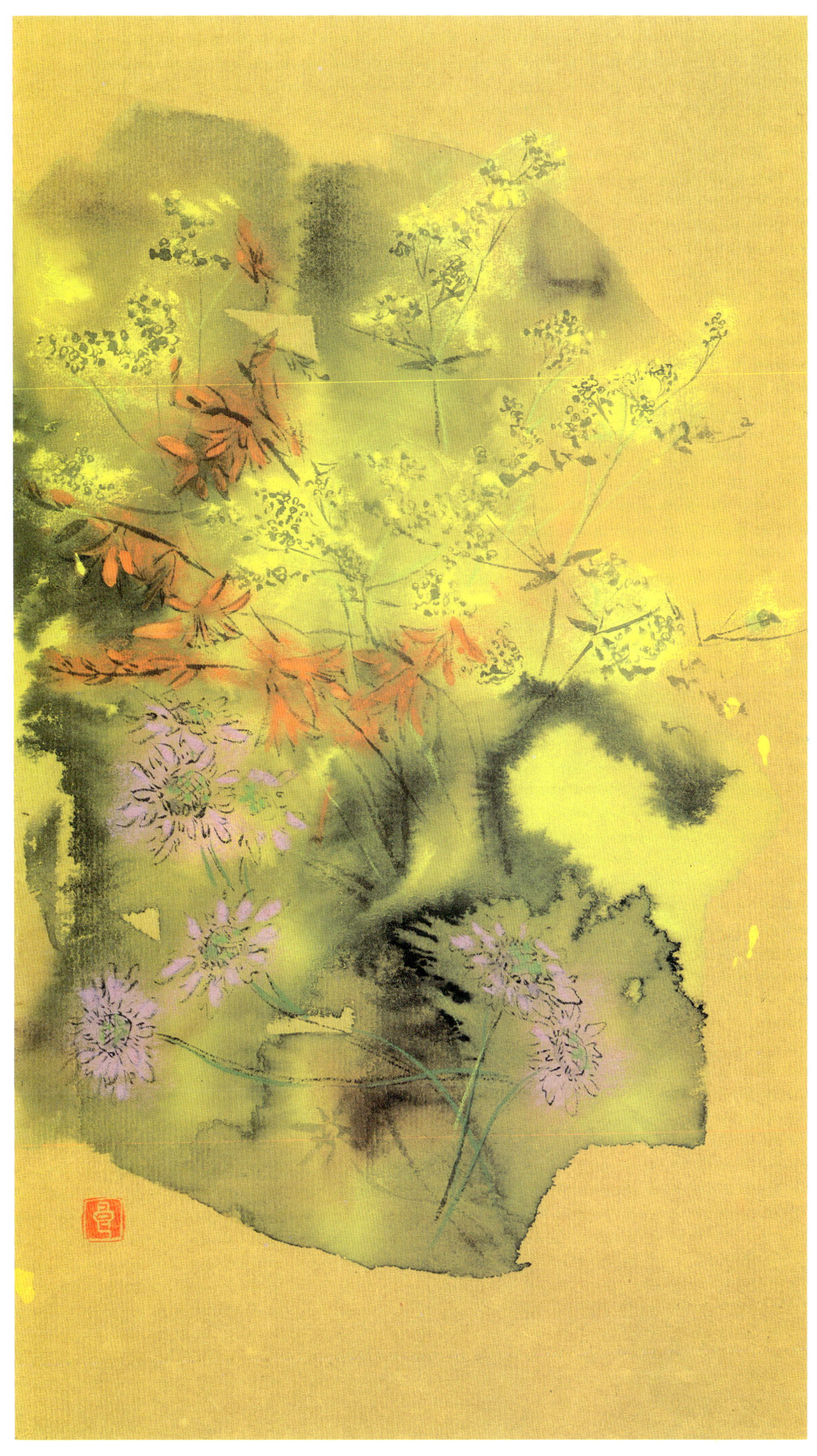

33

Cherry and Peach Flowers

1992. Tapestry. 51 1/4 × 63 inches. 130 × 160 cm.

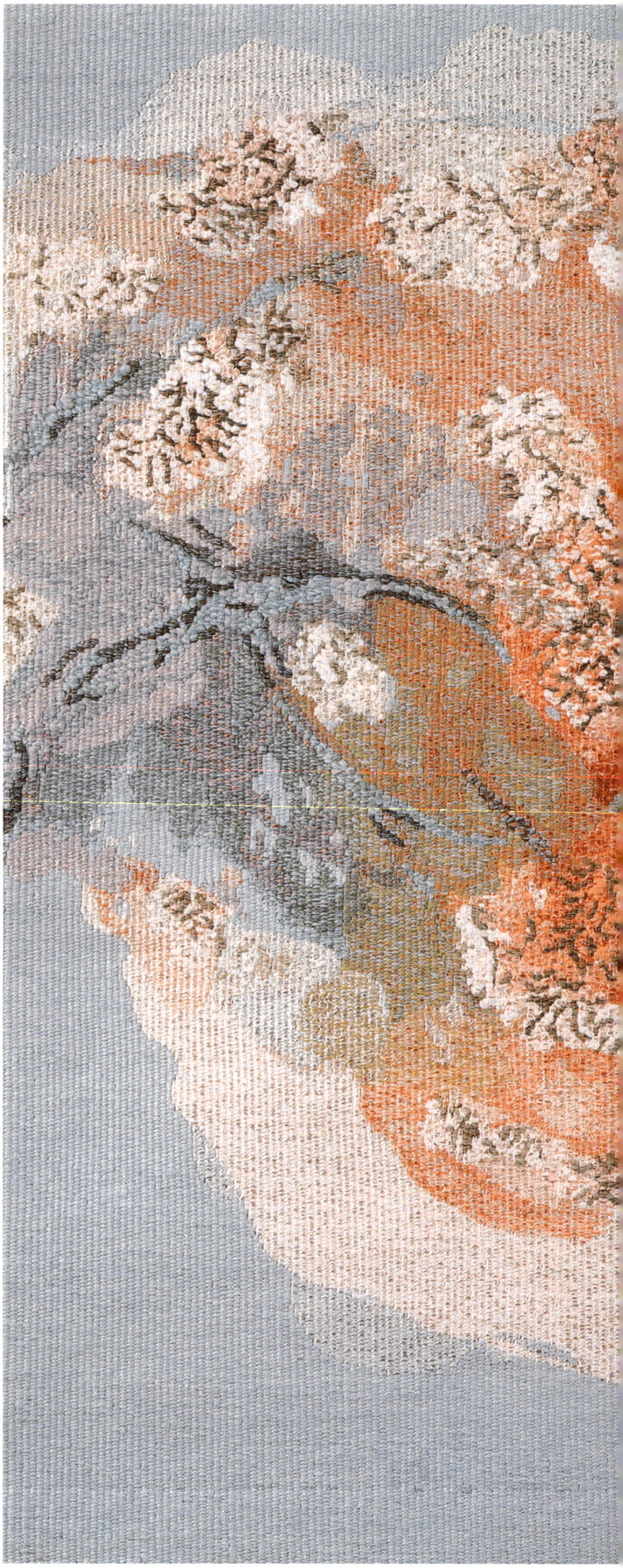

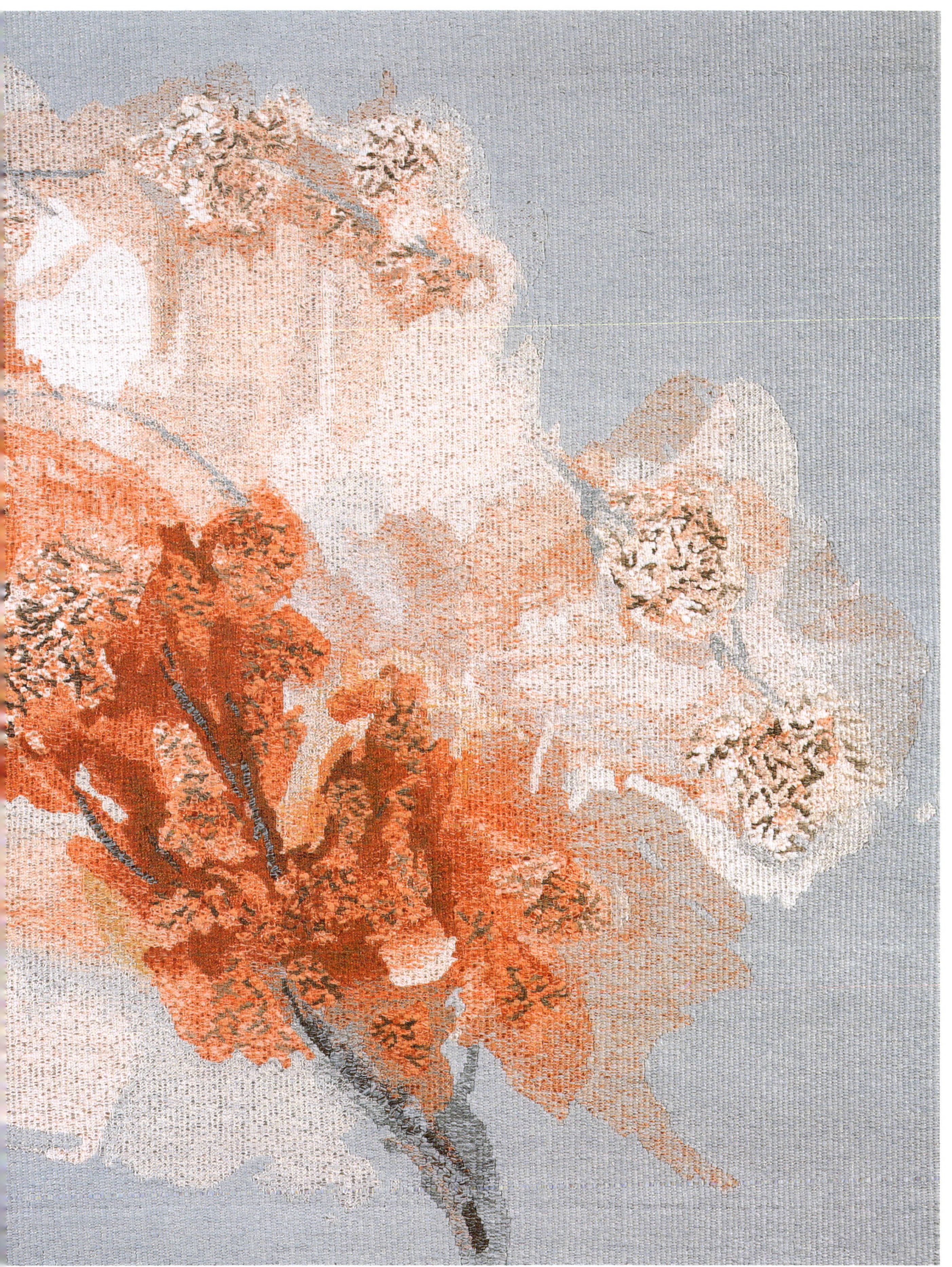

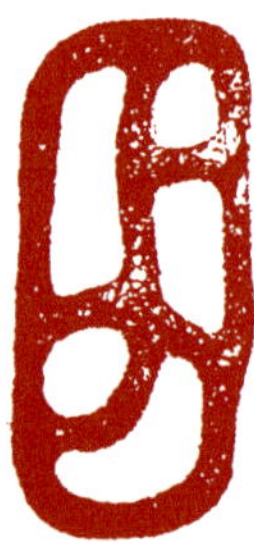

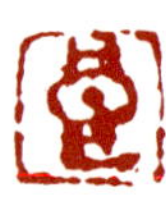

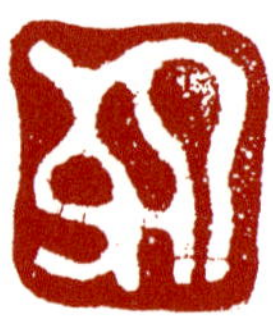

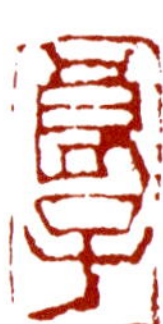

The artist's seal for pastel works

Exhibition Checklist

Chronology

Books Illustrated by Yoshiko Ishikawa

Exhibition Checklist

1
Winter (Icy Lake)
1984
Oil on canvas
78 3/4 × 39 3/8 inches. 200 × 100 cm.

2
Winter (Flowers in the Snow)
1984
Oil on canvas
78 3/4 × 39 3/8 inches. 200 × 100 cm.

3
Winter (Deep Snow)
1984
Oil on canvas
78 3/4 × 39 3/8 inches. 200 × 100 cm.

4
Spring (Amaryllis)
1984
Oil on canvas
78 3/4 × 39 3/8 inches. 200 × 100 cm.

5
Spring (Cherry Blossoms at Night)
1984
Oil on canvas
78 3/4 × 39 3/8 inches. 200 × 100 cm.

6
Spring (Floral Streamer)
1984
Oil on canvas
78 3/4 × 39 3/8 inches. 200 × 100 cm.

7
Rain (Mt. Yoshino)
1984
Oil on canvas
70 7/8 × 70 7/8 inches. 180 × 180 cm.

8
Cherry Blossoms at Twilight
1988
Oil on canvas
59 1/8 × 31 1/2 inches. 150 × 80 cm.

9
Flower Life—A Lapse
1992
Six-panel folding screen
Oil on canvas
39 3/8 × 141 3/4 inches. 100 × 360 cm.

10
Double Cherry Blossoms (Fugenzo)
1992
Oil on canvas
39 3/8 × 39 3/8 inches. 100 × 100 cm.

11
Flurry of Blossoms
1982
Oil on canvas
39 3/8 × 23 5/8 inches. 100 × 60 cm.

12
Wind (Flurry of Cherry Blossoms)
1984
Oil on canvas
70 7/8 × 70 7/8 inches. 180 × 180 cm.

13
Flowery Clusters
1988
Oil on canvas
59 1/8 × 31 1/2 inches. 150 × 80 cm.

14
Ninnaji Temple
1992
Six-panel folding screen
Oil on canvas
39 3/8 × 141 3/4 inches. 100 × 360 cm.

15
Evening Sunglow
1992
Oil on canvas
39 3/8 × 39 3/8 inches. 100 × 100 cm.

16
Early Spring (Magnolia)
1990
Oil on canvas
59 1/8 × 31 1/2 inches. 150 × 80 cm.

17
Early Spring (Fern)
1990
Oil on canvas
59 1/8 × 31 1/2 inches. 150 × 80 cm.

18
After Rain
1990
Oil on canvas
59 1/8 × 27 1/2 inches. 150 × 70 cm.

19
Flurry of Blossoms
1980
Pastel, gouache and Chinese ink on paper
20 1/8 × 19 1/4 inches. 51 × 49 cm.

20
Double Cherry Blossoms (A)
1992
Pastel, gouache and Chinese ink on paper
25 3/8 × 8 1/8 inches. 64.5 × 20.5 cm.

21
Double Cherry Blossoms (B)
1992
Pastel, gouache and Chinese ink on paper
25 × 13 1/2 inches. 63.5 × 34.5 cm.

22
Anemone
1984
Pastel, gouache and Chinese ink on paper
20 1/8 × 17 1/4 inches. 51 × 44 cm.

23
Columbine
1990
Pastel, gouache and Chinese ink on paper
18 1/2 × 12 5/8 inches. 47 × 32 cm.

24
June Flowers
1984
Pastel, gouache and Chinese ink on paper
18 1/8 × 23 5/8 inches. 46 × 60 cm.

25
Hydrangea
1980
Pastel, gouache and Chinese ink on paper
20 1/2 × 22 1/4 inches. 52 × 56.5 cm.

26
Orchid
1984
Pastel, gouache and Chinese ink on paper
15 3/4 × 23 5/8 inches. 40 × 60 cm.

27
Black Lily
1984
Pastel, gouache and Chinese ink on paper
12 1/4 × 18 1/8 inches. 31 × 46 cm.

28
Chinese Bellflower
1978
Pastel, gouache and Chinese ink on paper
21 1/8 × 30 3/4 inches. 53.5 × 78 cm.

29
Alpine Flowers
1979
Pastel, gouache and Chinese ink on paper
17 1/4 × 19 3/4 inches. 44 × 50 cm.

30
Aconite
1990
Pastel, gouache and Chinese ink on paper
15 3/4 × 12 3/4 inches. 40 × 32.5 cm.

31
Amaryllis
1980
Pastel, gouache and Chinese ink on paper
19 3/4 × 9 1/2 inches. 50 × 24 cm.

32
Feminine Flowers
1990
Pastel, gouache and Chinese ink on paper
18 3/4 × 11 inches. 47.5 × 28 cm.

33
Cherry and Peach Flowers
1992
Tapestry
51 1/4 × 63 inches. 130 × 160 cm.

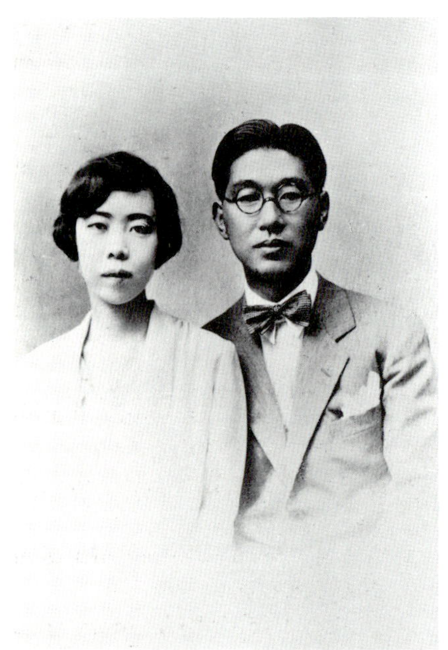
Her parents, Rome 1927

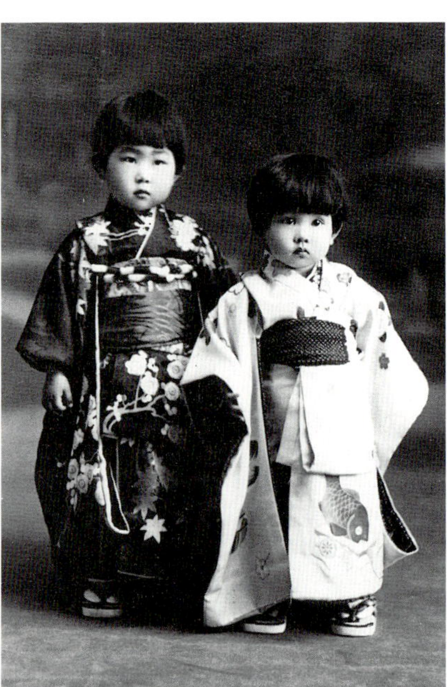
Yoshiko (right) with her sister, 1932

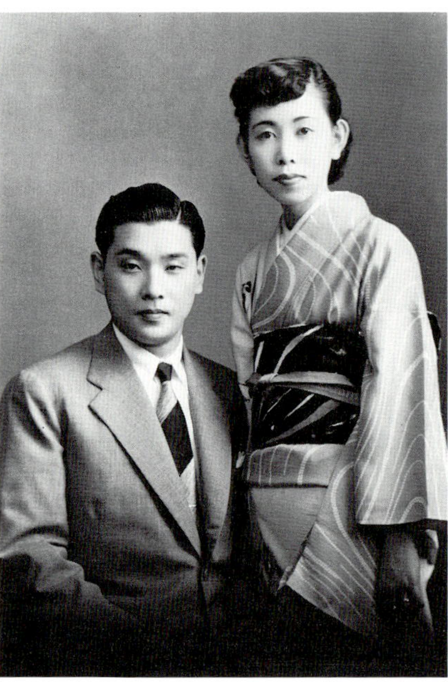
With her husband, 1953

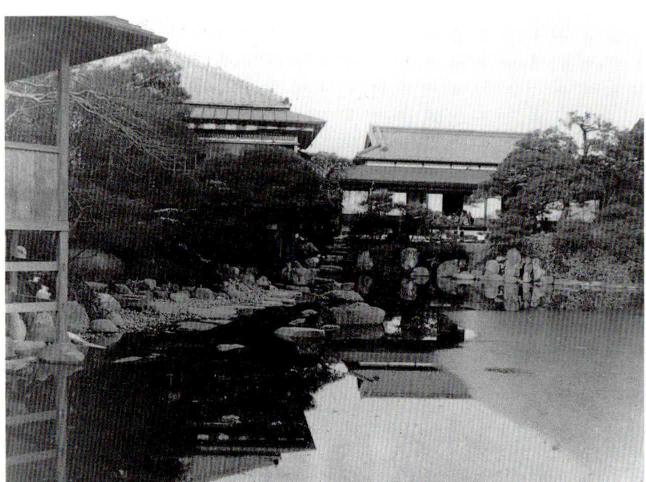
The Kajima estate, in which her mother was born, Tokyo (destroyed by the Great Earthquake of 1923)

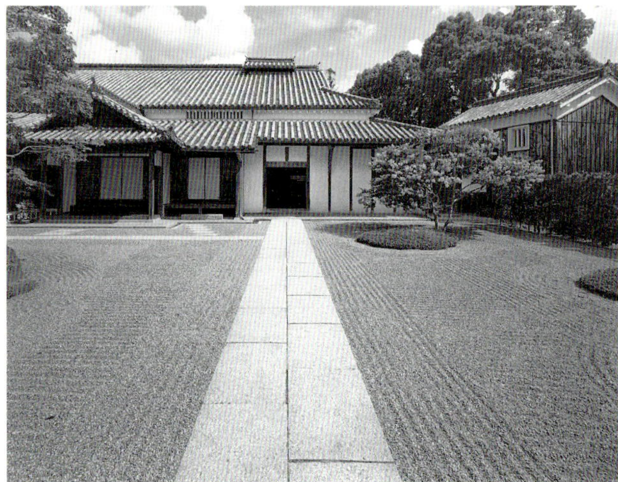
The Nagatomi estate, Hyogo Prefecture 1953

Chronology

1929 (showa 4) Born in Rome on April 5. Second daughter of Japanese diplomat Morinosuke Kajima and his wife, Ume, then on assignment in Italy.

1937 (showa 12) Studies privately with painter Saburo Kurata.

1946 (showa 21) Enters Japan Women's University, studying in the Department of Art History.

Studies privately with painter Satoe Arima.

1948 (showa 23) Completes 14 oils on the theme of the *Stations of the Cross*, Commissioned by the Reverend Satoshi Nagae, bishop of Saint Mary's Church, Tokyo.

1949 (showa 24) Studies privately with painter Sakujiro Okubo.

1950 (showa 25) Graduates from Japan Women's University. Thesis topic: "Landscape Sketches in the Venetian School of Painting."

1952 (showa 27) Oil *Garden Zinnia* accepted for eighth Nitten Exhibition for the first time.

1953 (showa 28) Marries Rokuro Ishikawa, son of the Chairman of the Federation of Economic Organizations, Ichiro Ishikawa.

1965 (showa 40) Oil *Pansies* included in ninth Yasui Award Exhibition, The National Museum of Modern Art, Tokyo.

1966 (showa 41) First solo exhibition at Nihonbashi Gallery, Tokyo (15 oils; 14 pastels).

1967 (showa 42) Oil *Amaryllis* included in eleventh Yasui Award Exhibition, The National Museum of Modern Art, Tokyo.

1968 (showa 43) Solo exhibition at Nihonbashi Gallery, Tokyo (11 oils; 13 pastels).

Illustrates English edition of *The Works of Busho, the Poet* by prominent Meiji Period poet Busho Sanjin, autonym Toshio Nagatomi, the artist's paternal grandfather. The Nagatomis is an ancient family, including the mother of Zeami, a famous Muromachi period (14th century) Noh playwright. The Nagatomi estate, in which father Morinosuke was born, has been designated an Important Cultural Asset.

1969 (showa 44) Oil *Hydrangea* included in eighth Exposition internationale du figuratif, Mitsukoshi Department Store, Nihonbashi, Tokyo.

1970 (showa 45) Oil *Orchid* (*A*) included in ninth Exposition internationale du figuratif, Mitsukoshi Department Store, Nihonbashi, Tokyo.

1971 (showa 46) Oil *Orchid* (*B*) included in tenth Exposition internationale du figuratif, Mitsukoshi Department Store, Nihonbashi, Tokyo.

1973 (showa 48) Solo exhibition at Saiko-do Gallery, Tokyo (8 oils; 22 pastels).

1975 (showa 50) Solo exhibition at Tokyo Central Gallery, Tokyo (15 oils; 21 pastels).

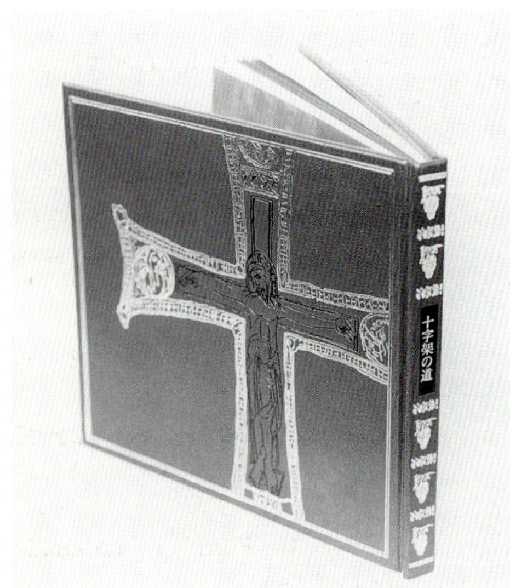

Catalogue, *Stations of the Cross*, 1976

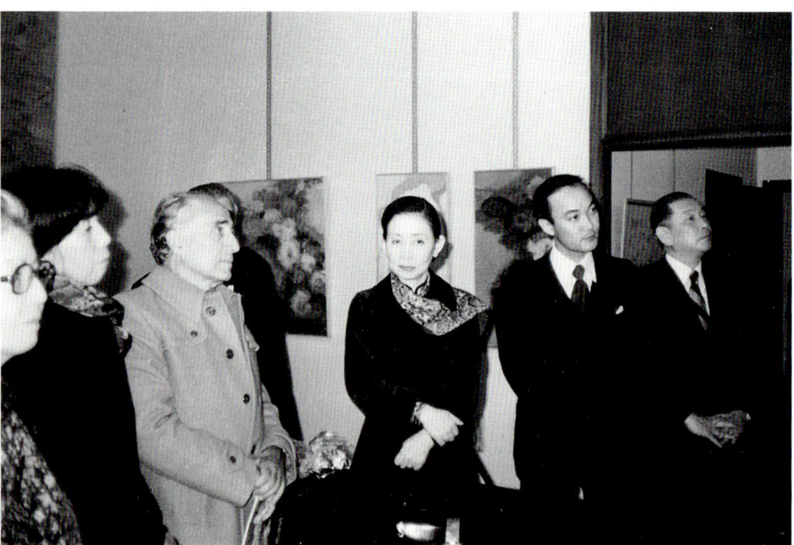

Solo exhibition at Toninelli Arte Moderna, Rome 1978
(with sculptor Emilio Greco)

Gazzetta del Sud

mostre d'arte

Yoshiko Ishikawa

Newspaper article about her exhibition in Rome, 1978

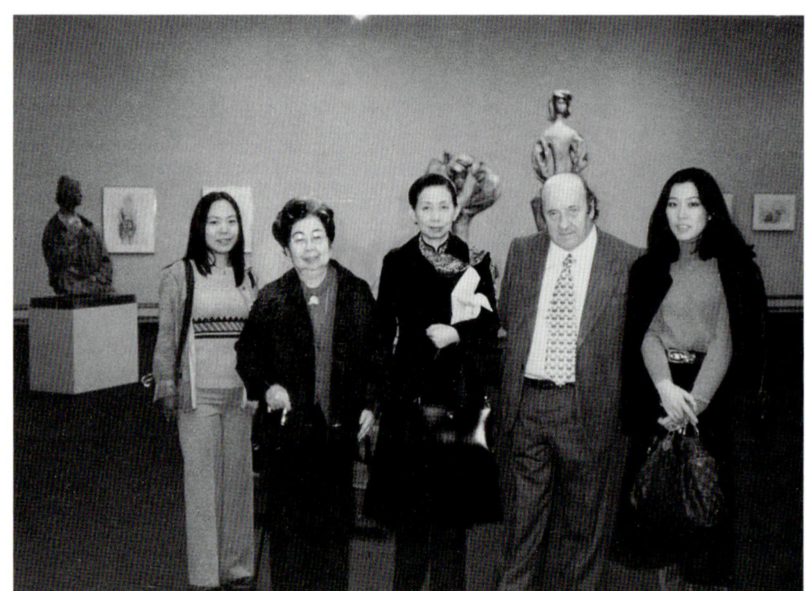

Visiting sculptor Giacomo Manzù, Rome 1978
(with her mother and daughter)

1976 (showa 51) Named to Board of Trustees of the Kajima Foundation.

Publishes Stations of the Cross collection in book dedicated to her father, who died December 3, 1975.

1977 (showa 52) Solo exhibition at Tokyo Central Gallery, Tokyo (17 oils; 18 pastels).

1978 (showa 53) Oils *Gladiolas*, *Garden Zinnia* and *Tiger Lilies* included in La Foire internationale d'art contemporain (FIAC), Grand Palais, Paris.

Solo exhibition at Toninelli Arte Moderna, Rome (16 oils; 20 pastels).

1979 (showa 54) Solo exhibition at Toninelli Arte Moderna, Milano (16 oils; 20 pastels).

Solo exhibition at Palazzo Corvaja, Taormina, Sicily (16 oils; 20 pastels).

Receives Taormina Art Award.

Oils *Rain*, *Wind* and *Flower* included in La Foire internationale d'art contemporain (FIAC), Grand Palais, Paris.

Oil *Orchid* included in Panorama 79, Tokyo Central Annex, Tokyo.

1980 (snowa 55) Oils *Bamboo (Shoot)*, *Bamboo (Youth)* and *Bamboo (Prime)* included in La Foire internationale d'art contemporain (FIAC), Grand Palais, Paris.

Oil *Poppies* included in Panorama 80, Tokyo Central Annex, Tokyo.

1981 (showa 56) Solo exhibition at Tokyo Central Annex, Tokyo (20 oils; 30 pastels).

Oil *Flowers of the Nile* included in first Exhibition of Women Painters, Takashimaya Department Store, Nihonbashi, Tokyo.

Oils *Autumn (Leaves Searing Blast)*, *Autumn (Flowery Flame)* and *Autumn (Late Chrysanthemum)* included in La Foire internationale d'art contemporain (FIAC), Grand Palais, Paris.

Oil *Summer (Cool Breeze)* included in second Contemporary Women's Art Exhibition, The Ueno Royal Museum, Tokyo.

Oil *Camellia* included in Panorama 81, Tokyo Central Annex, Tokyo.

Oils *Spring on the Nile*, *In the Rainy Season (A)* and *In the Rainy Season (B)* included in twentyth Exposition internationale du figuratif, Mitsukoshi Department Store, Nihonbashi, Tokyo.

1982 (showa 57) Oil *Flower* included in ARCO exhibition, Madrid.

Oil *Flurry of Blossoms* included in second Exhibition of Women Painters, Takashimaya Department Store, Nihonbashi, Tokyo.

La «Targa speciale» alla pittrice dei fiori

E' stata assegnata a Yoshiko Ishikawa -- La targa «Città di Taormina» al sen. Oscar Andò

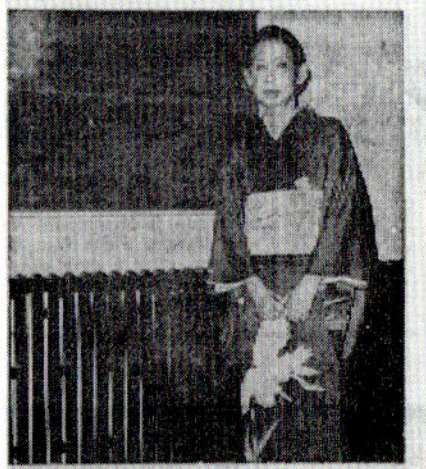

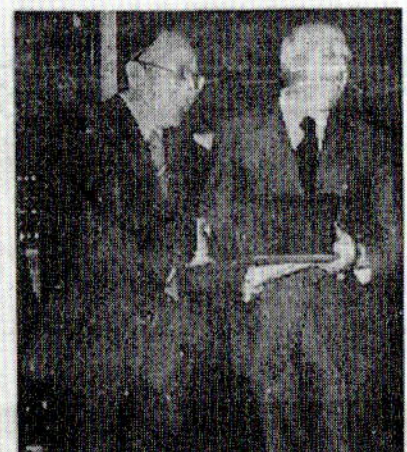

La pittrice Yoshiko Ishikawa e il sen. Andò mentre riceve il premio. (Foto Spadoni)

Nostro servizio particolare

TAORMINA, 18 giugno

Yoshiko Ishikawa, la pittrice giapponese che espone sino al 30 giugno a Palazzo Corvaja, ha ricevuto, giungendo per la prima volta in Sicilia, la «Targa speciale» nel corso della cerimonia di consegna dei «premi Taormina per le arti e le scienze», istituite dal locale Lions Club.

La delicata pittrice dei fiori il giorno successivo, ha inteso ringraziare la città che la ospita con un cocktail al quale hanno preso parte numerose autorità, tra cui il sottosegretario on. Azzaro, il prefetto di Messina dott. Vitarelli, il vicepresidente dell'A R S Salvatore D'Alia e l'ambasciatore Francesco Paolo Fulci. Tra gli invitati anche il senatore Oscar Andò che dalle mani del sindaco Turiano ha ricevuto, nel corso della stessa manifestazione lionistica, la «Targa Città di Taormina».

Il meritato riconoscimento al senatore Andò va ricollegato al suo appassionato e civile impegno per la realizzazione dell'autostrada Messina - Catania, del cui Consorzio fu primo presidente. La motivazione ha sottolineato infatti, l'intuito dell'uomo politico messinese circa l'enorme valore socio economico e turistico di un più rapido collegamento tra le due città di Messina e di Catania.

G. D. B.

Newspaper article about her exhibition in Taormina, Sicily 1979

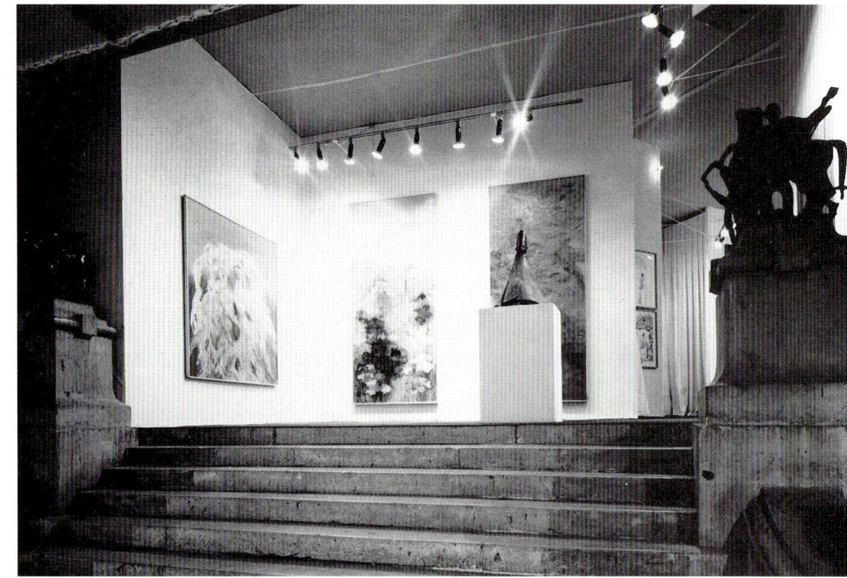

FIAC, Grand Palais, Paris 1979

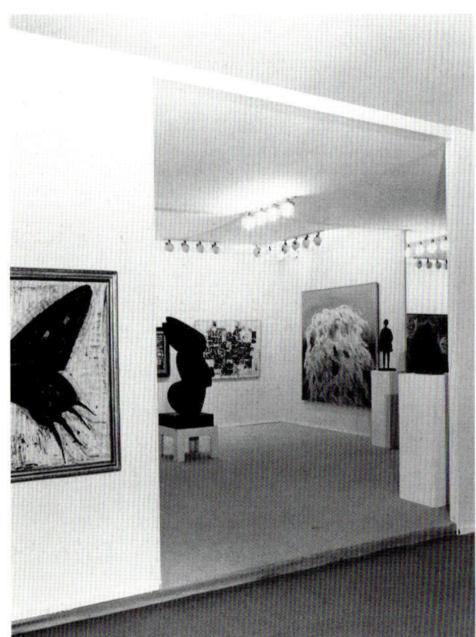

Her exhibit (right in the back) at ARCO, Madrid 1982

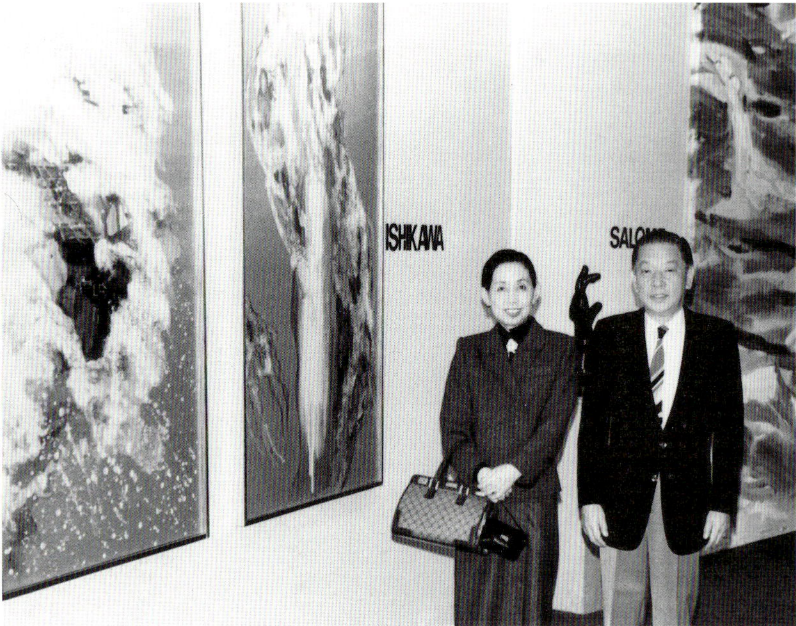

With her husband at FIAC, Grand Palais, Paris 1983

Oil *Forest Sunshine* included in third Contemporary Women's Art Exhibition, The Ueno Royal Museum, Tokyo.

Oil *Bamboo* (*Youth*) developed into tapestry by Tatsumura Textile Co. and hung in Senmaya City Hall, Iwate Prefecture.

Oil *Spindle Flower* included in Panorama 82, Tokyo Central Annex, Tokyo.

Named to Board of Trustees of the Kajima Foundation for the Arts.

1983 (showa 58) Oils *Flurry of Blossoms*, *Summer* (*Cool Breeze*) and *Summer* (*Brook*) included in Salone Internazionale Mercanti d'Arte (SIMA), Palazzo Grassi, Venice.

Oil *Wisteria Flowers* included in third Exhibition of Women Painters, Takashimaya Department Store, Nihonbashi, Tokyo.

Oils *Spring* (*Cherry Blossoms at Night*) and *Spring* (*Floral Streamer*) included in La Foire internationale d'art contemporain (FIAC), Grand Palais, Paris.

Oil *Autumn* (*Late Chrysanthemum*) included in fourth Contemporary Women's Art Exhibition, The Ueno Royal Museum, Tokyo.

Oil *Chrysanthemum* included in Panorama 83, Tokyo Central Annex, Tokyo.

1984 (showa 59) Solo exhibition at Tokyo Central Annex, Tokyo (11 oils; 13 pastels).

Oil *Spring* (*Cherry Blossoms at Night*) included in fifth Contemporary Women's Art Exhibition, The Ueno Royal Museum, Tokyo.

1985 (showa 60) Prints *Cherry Blossom* (*A*) and *Cherry Blossom* (*B*) presented to Hotel Bellevue, Dresden.

Oil *Autumn Garden* included in sixth Contemporary Women's Art Exhibition, The Ueno Royal Museum, Tokyo.

1986 (showa 61) Oil *Flowers of Sydney* included in fifth Exhibition of Women Painters, Takashimaya Department Store, Nihonbashi, Tokyo.

Oil *Flowers of Palau* included in twenty-fifth Exposition internationale du figuratif, Mitsukoshi Department Store, Nihonbashi, Tokyo.

Oil *Alpine Flowers* included in seventh Contemporary Women's Art Exhibition, The Ueno Royal Museum, Tokyo.

1987 (showa 62) Oil *Flowers of Jacaranda* in sixth Exhibition of Women Painters, Takashimaya Department Store, Nihonbashi, Tokyo.

Oils *Orchids* (*A*) and *Orchids* (*B*) and two works painted in collabo-

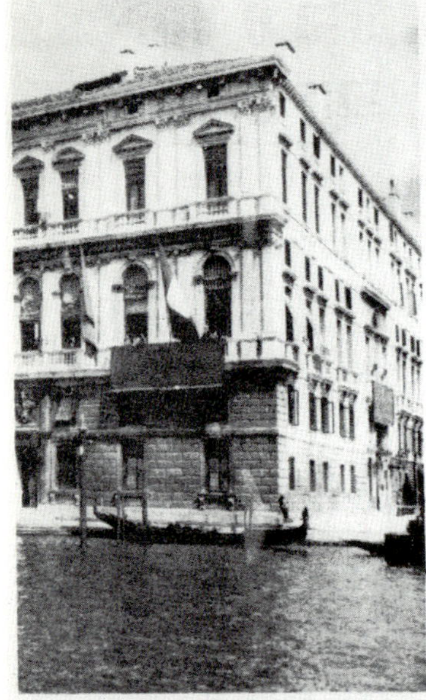

L'ARTE A PALAZZO GRASSI

La prima edizione del salone internazionale dei mercanti d'arte promossa dal centro di cultura di palazzo Grassi, a Venezia, è stata aperta ufficialmente ieri dal ministro per i rapporti con il parlamento, Abis.

Il ministro Abis, accompagnato dal ministro per le partecipazioni statali Gianni De Michelis, e dal presidente del centro di palazzo Grassi, Mario Valeri Manera, ha quindi visitato la mostra. Nelle sale del palazzo del Massari sono esposte circa 800 opere dei maggiori artisti del nostro tempo.

Newspaper article about SIMA, Venice 1983

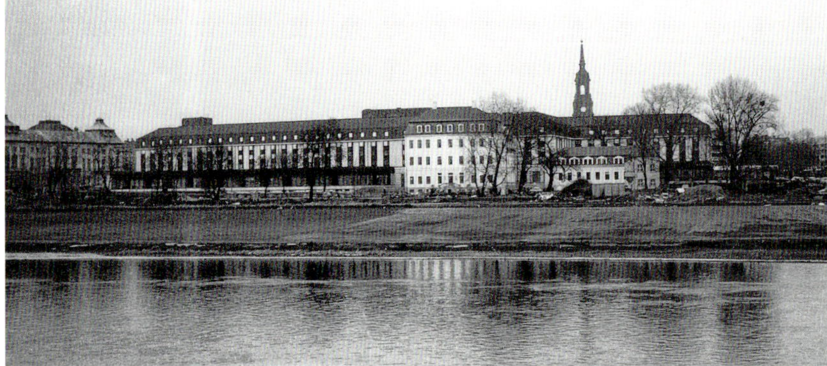

Hotel Bellevue, Dresden 1985

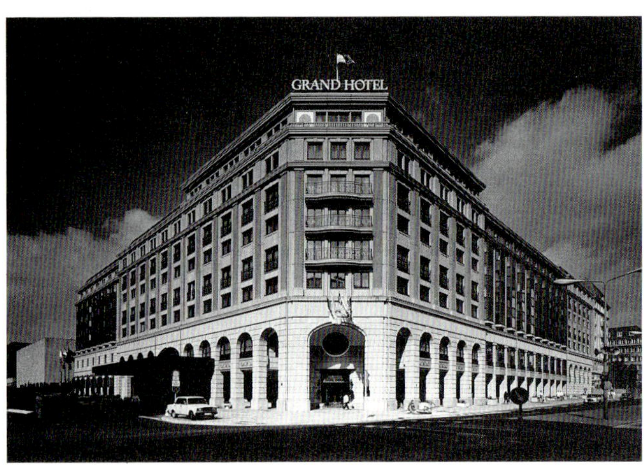

Grand Hotel, Berlin 1987

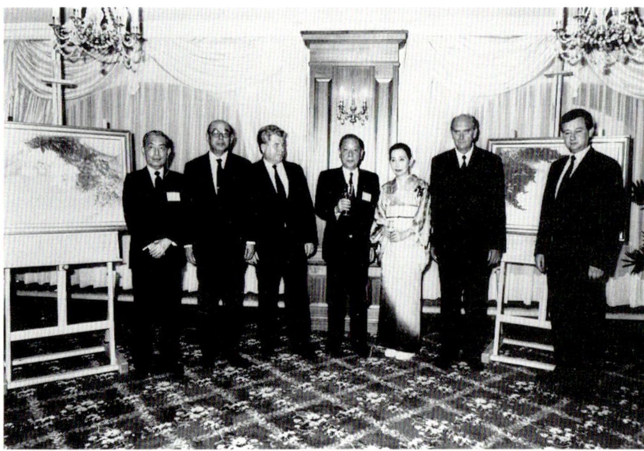

At Grand Hotel, Berlin 1987

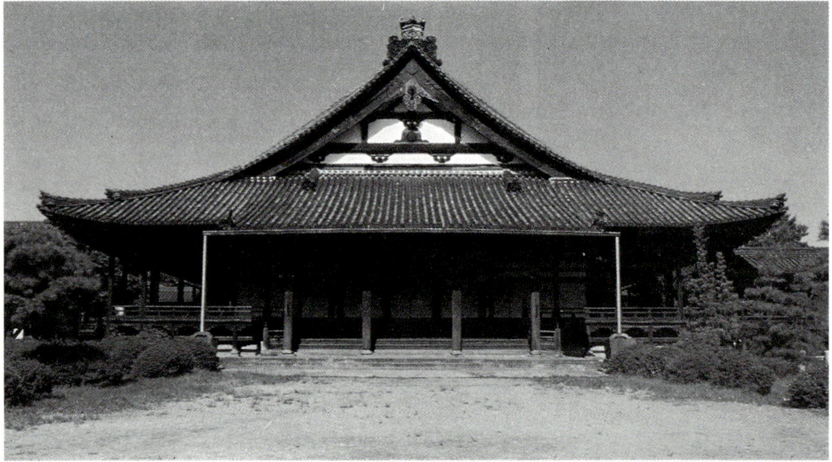

Kameyama-Hontokuji Temple, Hyogo Prefecture 1991

ration with calligrapher Takako Ohishi — *Tokyo* and *Kyoto* — presented to the Grand Hotel, Berlin.

Oil *Bushes* included in eighth Contemporary Women's Art Exhibition, The Ueno Royal Museum, Tokyo.

1988 (showa 63) Oil *Withered Ferns* included in seventh Exhibition of Women Painters, Takashimaya Department Store, Nihonbashi, Tokyo.

Oil *Flowery Clusters* included in ninth Contemporary Women's Art Exhibition, The Ueno Royal Museum, Tokyo.

1989 (heisei 1) Oil *Cherry Blossoms at Twilight* included in eighth Exhibition of Women Painters, Takashimaya Department Store, Nihonbashi, Tokyo.

Oil *Cogongrasses* included in tenth Contemporary Women's Art Exhibition, The Ueno Royal Museum, Tokyo.

1990 (heisei 2) Oil *Autumn Wisteria* included in ninth Exhibition of Women Painters, Takashimaya Department Store, Nihonbashi, Tokyo.

Solo exhibition at Galerie Nichido, Tokyo (24 oils; 24 pastels; 2 lithographs; 4 etchings).

Oil *Afterglow* purchased by Setagaya Art Museum, Tokyo.

Oil *After Rain* included in eleventh Contemporary Women's Art Exhibition, The Ueno Royal Museum, Tokyo.

1991 (heisei 3) Oil *Golden Leaves* included in tenth Exhibition of Women Painters, Takashimaya Department Store, Nihonbashi, Tokyo.

Commissioned by Renshi Ohtani Shosei, Head Priest of the Kameyama Hontokuji Temple, Hyogo Prefecture, to paint 85 panels in the classical style for the temple's Grand Ceremony Hall, designated an Important Cultural Asset.

Oil *In the Rainy Season* included in twelveth Contemporary Women's Art Exhibition, The Ueno Royal Museum, Tokyo.

Early Spring (*Violets*) developed into a tapestry by Tatsumura Textile Co. commissioned by The Meiji Mutual Life Insurance Co.

1992 (heisei 4) Oil *Summer's End* included in eleventh Exhibition of Women Painters, Takashimaya Department Store, Nihonbashi, Tokyo.

Oil *Cherry and Peach Flowers* developed into a tapestry by Tatsumura Textile Co.

1993 (heisei 5) Solo exhibition *Sakura: Cherry Blossom Paintings by Yoshiko Ishikawa* presented at The National Museum of Women in the Arts, Washington, D.C. (18 oils; 14 pastels; 1 tapestry).

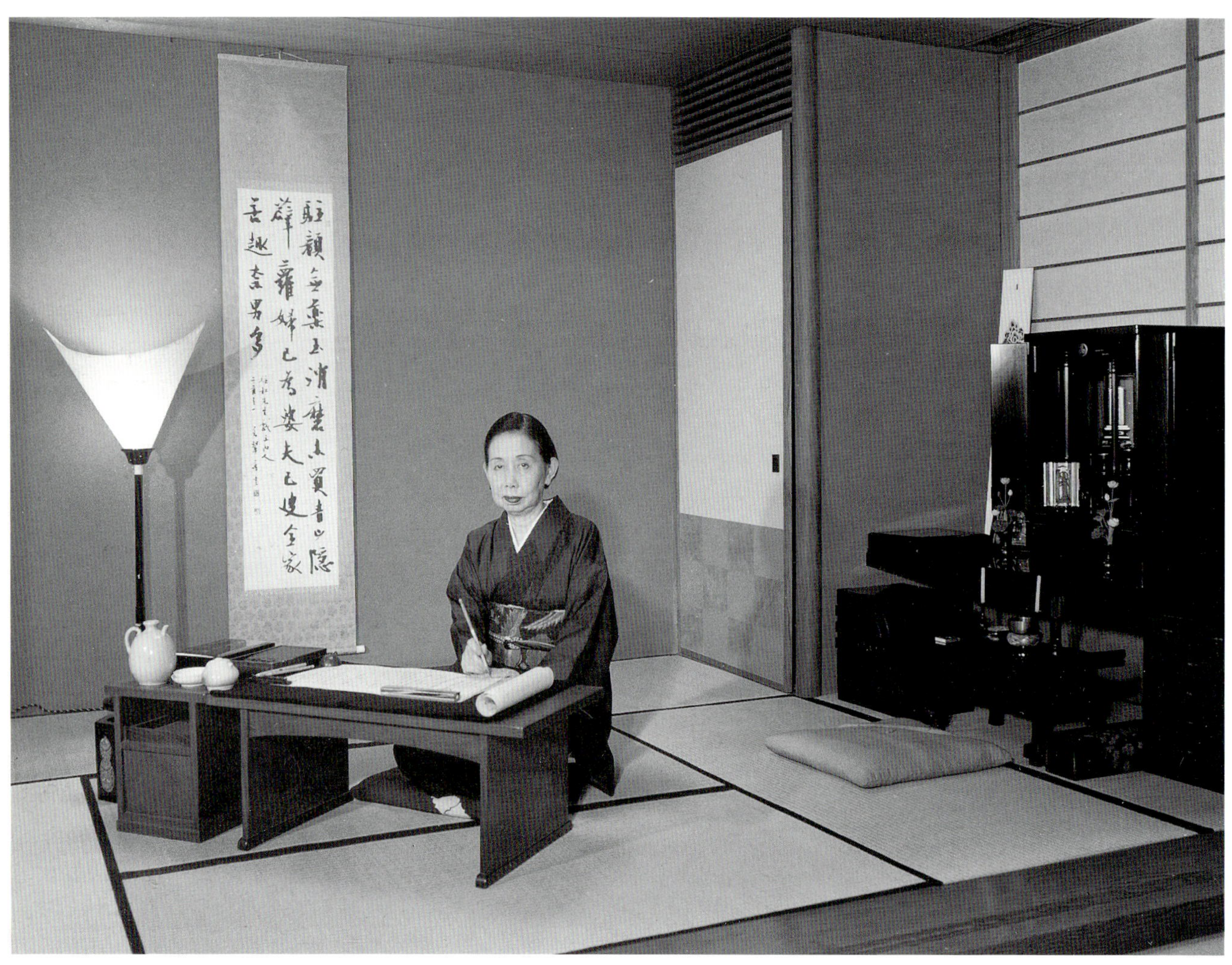

In her atelier, Tokyo 1992

Books Illustrated by Yoshiko Ishikawa

1968 *Young Ladies, to You.* (*In commemoration of receiving the Second Kajima Peace Award*) by Kaoru Hatoyama. Tokyo: Kajima Institute Publishing.

1979 *The Vacant Room* by Ayako Sono. Tokyo: Bungeishunju.

Today is Gone to the Sea by Ayako Sono. Kodansha Literary Collection. Tokyo: Kodansha.

Standing in the Afterglow by Ayako Sono. Bunshun Literary Collection. Tokyo: Bungeishunju.

God's Puppet: The Spiritual World of Ayako Sono by Nobuko Tsuruha. Tokyo: Shufunotomo.

Vanishing Footsteps by Ayako Sono. Bunshun Literary Collection. Tokyo: Bungeishunju.

1980 *The Structure of Youth* by Ayako Sono. Bunshun Literary Collection. Tokyo: Bungeishunju.

Nurtured by the Land by Ayako Sono. Kodansha Literary Collection. Tokyo: Kodansha.

Red Plum, White Plum by Ayako Sono. Kodansha Literary Collection. Tokyo: Kodansha.

1981 *An Afternoon Smile* by Ayako Sono. New edition. Tokyo: The Mainichi Newspapers.

Father Cimatti, Like Sun in the Sky by A. Crevacore. Tokyo: Don Bosco Press.

1982 *A Record of Aging: On Saving Oneself* by Ayako Sono. New edition. Tokyo: Shodensha.

Special edition Bungei Shunju (no.161). Tokyo: Bungeishunju.

1984 *Letters to Mother: Father Kolbe, the Saint of Auschwitz* by Maximiliano Kolbe. Translated by Tatsuya Nishiyama. Nagasaki: Seibo No Kishi Sha.

1985 *Why Me? A Woman of Samaria* by Noboru Yoshiyama. Nagasaki: Seibo No Kishi Sha.

1987 *Days of Barely Being Me* by Ayako Sono. Shueisha Literary Collection. Tokyo: Shueisha.

The Jihi Coast by Ayako Sono. Shueisha Literary Collection. Tokyo: Shueisha.

1988 *Until the Day of Parting: Letters of the Tokyo Vatican Restoration* by Ayako Sono and Masayuki Shirieda. Shinchosha Literary Collection. Tokyo: Shinchosha.

Husband and Wife: This Strange Relationship by Ayako Sono. PHP Institute Literary Collection. Kyoto: PHP

Showa History of Madame Saisho by Fuyuko Kamisaka. Tokyo: Bungeishunju.

1989 *In this World of Sorrow* by Ayako Sono. Kodansha Literary Collection. Tokyo: Kodansha.

1991 *Irozange* by Chiyo Uno. Shinchosha Literary Collection. Tokyo: Shinchosha.

1992 *Wives of the Financial World* by Fuyuko Kamisaka. Tokyo: Kodansha.

Setsuzo: Second Collection of Poems and Writings by Tomi Hasegawa. Tokyo: Kajima Institute Publishing.

Printed in Japan